The ENCHANTED APPLES of OZ

by ERIC SHANOWER

D0568539

Founded on and continuing the famous Oz stories of L. Frank Baum

To Margaret and Chris
for enchantment created.

FIRST GRAPHIC NOVEL

The Enchanted Apples of Oz
by Eric Shanower
First Graphic Novel Number Five

Copyright © 1986 First Comics, Inc.
Introduction copyright © 1986 The Kilimanjaro Corporation

All rights reserved, including the right to reproduce this book or portions thereof in any
form whatsoever.

The stories, incidents, and characters mentioned in this publication are entirely fictional.
No actual persons, living or dead, without satiric intent, are intended or should be inferred
(or even theorized). The Enchanted Apples of Oz, Valynn, Bortag, and Drox are trademarks
of First Comics, Inc.

Published by First Comics, Inc.
435 N. LaSalle Street
Chicago, IL 60610

Rick Obadiah
  Publisher
Rick Oliver
  Editorial Director
Laurel Fitch
  Editorial Coordinator

Alex Wald
  Art Director
Rick Taylor
  Production Manager
Kathy Kotsivas
  Operations Director

Printed in the United States of America

ISBN: 0-915419-04-1

First Printing: April 1986

1 2 3 4 5 6 7 8 9 0

RANDOM REMARKS OF OZ

introduction by

HARLAN ELLISON

It's not that far a fetch, it only seems so; but during the three or four years that I spent in part lecturing around the United States in service of the Equal Rights Amendment, I took the name of Dorothy, the Small and Meek, if not in vain, surely to sincere purpose. From the speakers' platform I invoked the names of great women of the past as models for the women of today. Mary Wollstonecraft Shelley, Elizabeth Cady Stanton, Margaret Mead, Margaret Bourke-White, Sojourner Truth, Amelia Earhart, Eleanor Roosevelt. . . and Dorothy Gale of Kansas.

When the names of Joan of Arc or Madame Curie or even Charlotte Corday passed my lips, heads would nod appreciatively and I saw instant resonances for my listeners. But when Dorothy's name was presented, there would be the faintest beetling of brows, the telltale moue that indicated a difficulty in making ready connections.

So I would have to point out that even though Dorothy was a very young woman indeed, and despite her pronouncement that she was Small and Meek, the kid was a sensational role model for Our Times. Sensational, because she was bold, she was inventive, she was brave and competent and kind and loyal; she was quick to think on her feet, and she had a definite sense of purpose. Then the brows would smooth out, the smiles would appear, and I could move on to a discussion of why America *needed* the ERA.

(Sadly, the Wicked Witch of the West, Phyllis Schlafly, sent her flying monkeys against the ERA, and for a time now there has been darkness upon our land. But the Dorothys of this life haven't given up. There is always tomorrow. But that's a different story for a different time.)

What I never said, and I say it now hoping it'll be taken in the proper spirit, is that I also always thought Dorothy might be operating a few bricks short of a load. The kid wasn't quite right in her head, to be candid about it. I don't mean *actually* off her chump, like the people you meet every day who believe in flying saucers stuffed full of little green men, or those who enjoy the Smurfs, but just a headlight or two shy of full luminescence.

Let me put it this way: if *you* could live in Oz, with Munchkins and Quadlings and a Nome King and a Shaggy Man who speaks in verse, not to mention a Tin Woodman, a charming Scarecrow or a courageous Tik-Tok, would *you* get all psycho about going back to Kansas?

Kansas is a pleasant enough place. I've got many friends in Kansas, and KC jazz never grows wearying, and the Royals are a pretty fair ball team. But Kansas over Oz?!? Come *on!* Gimme a break here. That cyclone must have dropped her on her head, if she preferred Leavenworth or Coffeyville or Iola to The Emerald City.

That was, for me, through a childhood and adulthood of which the Oz books formed an important part, the one aspect of L. Frank Baum's miraculous canon that I could not accept. Well, yes, of course I understand that Dorothy's pathological need to return to dull, bland, gray Kansas in 1900 was a part of the moral substructure that underlay all the Oz books, as well as a necessary plot motivater — the classic Search for the Grail of all such traditional sagas — but everything else that Baum or those who followed him to take pen in hand set down was so wonderfully *believable*. Didn't matter if it was a Wishing Horse or Kalidahs or the Woggle-Bug or the Lovely Lady of Light, I accepted everything; without doubt, without problems of logic or the physical universe; I *believed*.

And so, if one believes in Oz (and I've never met anyone who didn't, from Ray Bradbury to Buckminster Fuller to Carl Sagan — all of whom Ozophiles), then one finally and sorrowfully has to come to the conclusion that Dorothy had to be *nuts* to want to leave that fascinating venue. Show me a man or woman who hasn't tried to figure out a way safely to cross the Deadly Desert, at least once in his or her life, and I'll show you a man or woman who had a deprived childhood.

Because of all the imaginary lands to which we have journeyed in books — from Barsoom to Xothique — the territories of Oz are surely the most congenial to children, and to those of us whom society dismisses as grown-up children. Oz casts a spell for anyone fresh enough in wonder to permit its magic to do its best. A spell deeper and stronger than just that of an MGM movie (or even a Disney sequel, which deserved far better than it received at the hands of *real* grown-ups, who shouldn't have been allowed to see it, because their hearts were as turned to stone as Valynn's body in the Oz book you now hold). Oz is as real to those of us who grew up with the books, as Wichita or Concordia or Emporia. And if we ever got the chance to take up residence there, it would take an army of Wheelers to evict us.

And that is why all true Ozophiles should greet Eric Shanower and his first *new* tale of the Land of Oz with open arms and open hearts. Mr. Baum left a legacy of joy and wonder that others have heightened and enriched, whether by the name Ruth Plumly Thompson or John R. Neill or Jack Snow or Rachel Cosgrove or March Laumer or Philip José Farmer or Onyx Madden. There is no question of "improper" historians of Oz, if the one telling the tale loves the originals and does not seek to "update" the canon with the introduction of modern troubles.

I did not know Mr. Shanower's work before I came to this new tale of Oz, but it is clear from the first that his heart is pure and his pen is sure. Just consider Bortag. There is dimension to him. He isn't the malevolent juggernaut of mischief a non-Ozophile would conjure up; he is a tragic creation, with a secret desire any one of us can credit and with which we can sympathize. Bortag is the kind of character Ruth Plumly Thompson would have approved. He looks like one thing, but he is quite another. And Eric Shanower made him up out of his own head. Not to mention Drox, the flying swordfish, who is the other really nifty new Ozian personality.

I commend Mr. Shanower to you, and I commend his work as being fully and truly in the mainstream of Ozmopolitan literature. But more, I urge you to draw Mr. Shanower's lovely conceits to your heart, because we can never get enough of the good stuff, the real stuff, in this frequently troubling, mischievous world filled with statesmen who dissemble, terrorists who maim, and comic book "auteurs" who think it's cute to show us men thrusting the barrels of .45's into women's mouths.

Ours is a time and a place that desperately needs to know that the beauty and wonder of Oz persists.

Mr. Baum and Miss Thompson are gone from us, but every now and then a new child-at-heart comes along to redraw the map . . . to whistle up the cyclone or call down the rainstorm that will carry us for a short time to Oz . . . where the dangers are great but are noble rather than debased. Where loyalty and quick-thinking and courage still count for much. Where straw men talk and chickens are clever.

A place where an Eric Shanower can sit under a magic apple tree and simply draw what he sees. Oh yes, I believe it: Mr. Shanower works from real life. And if we are very lucky, and you take him to your heart, he will bring back to us from that dear place ever more and better tales of the denizens of that magical kingdom so much more inviting
than Kansas.

Sorry, Dot.

Harlan Ellison

For more information on the world of Oz, write to:
The International Wizard of Oz Club
Fred M. Meyer, Executive Secretary
Box 95
Kinderhook, IL 62345

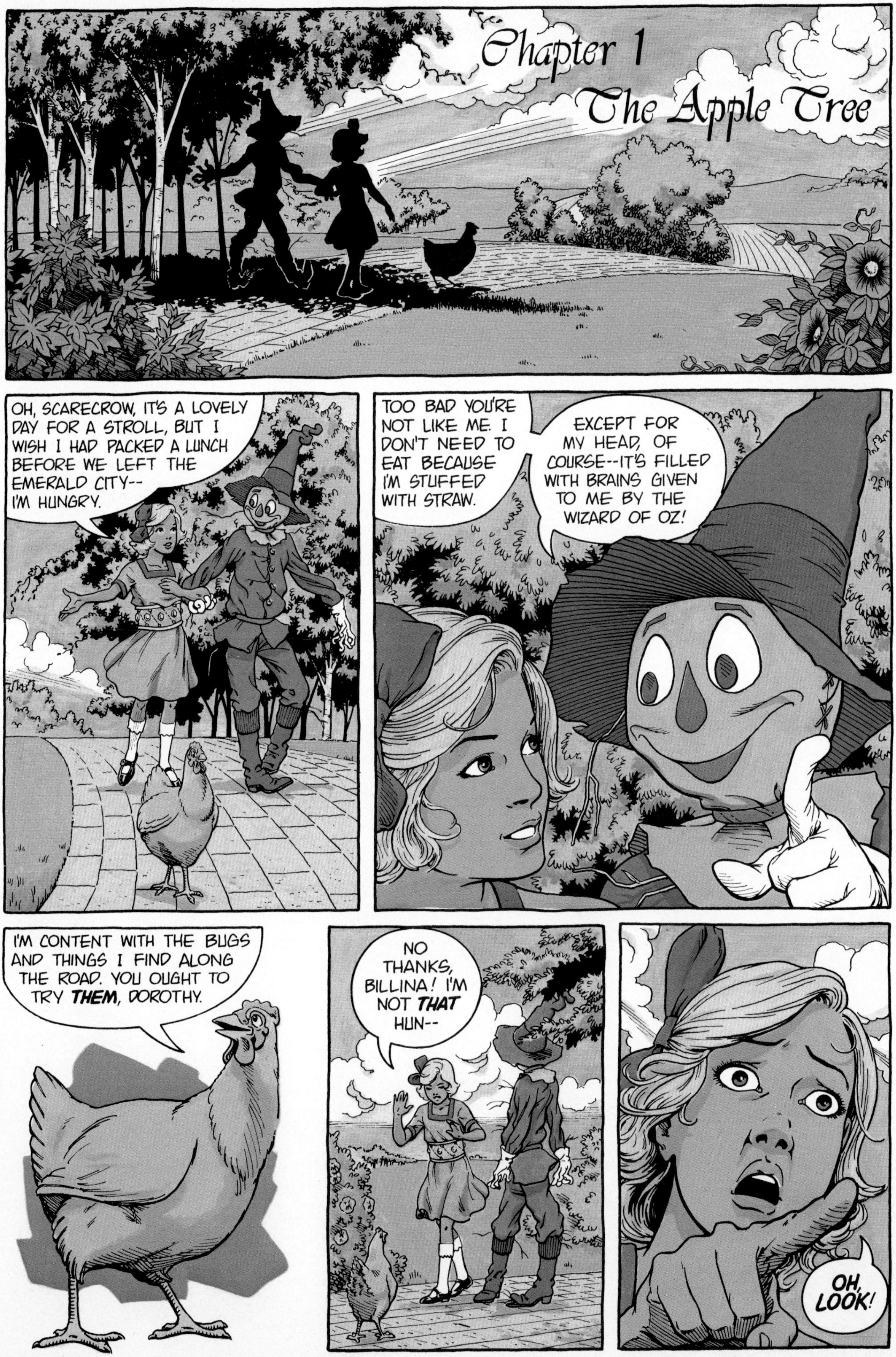

Chapter 1
The Apple Tree
OH, SCARECROW, IT'S A LOVELY DAY FOR A STROLL, BUT I WISH I HAD PACKED A LUNCH BEFORE WE LEFT THE EMERALD CITY-- I'M HUNGRY.
TOO BAD YOU'RE NOT LIKE ME. I DON'T NEED TO EAT BECAUSE I'M STUFFED WITH STRAW.
EXCEPT FOR MY HEAD, OF COURSE--IT'S FILLED WITH BRAINS GIVEN TO ME BY THE WIZARD OF OZ!
I'M CONTENT WITH THE BUGS AND THINGS I FIND ALONG THE ROAD. YOU OUGHT TO TRY **THEM**, DOROTHY.
NO THANKS, BILLINA! I'M NOT **THAT** HUN--
OH, LOOK!

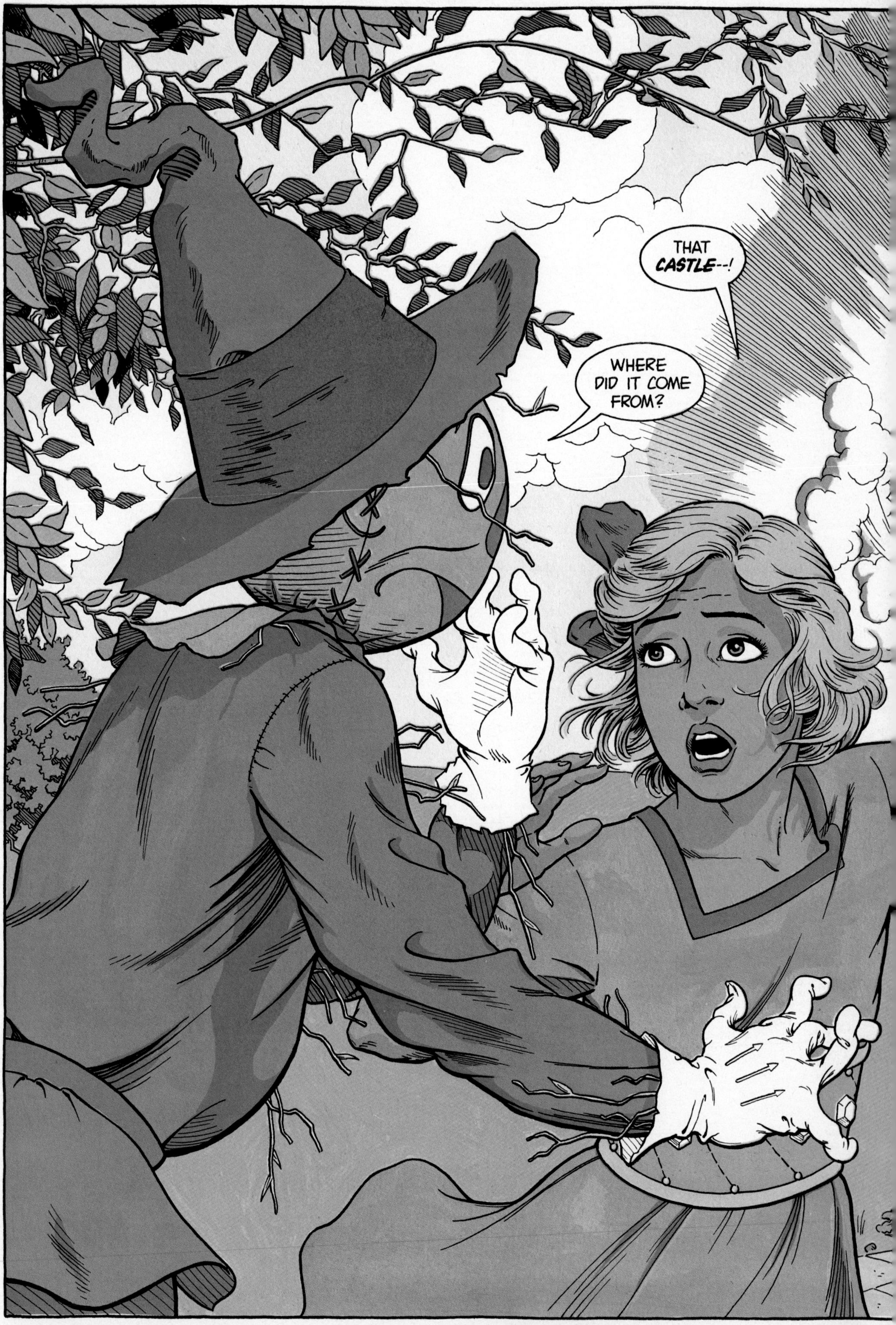
THAT CASTLE--!
WHERE DID IT COME FROM?

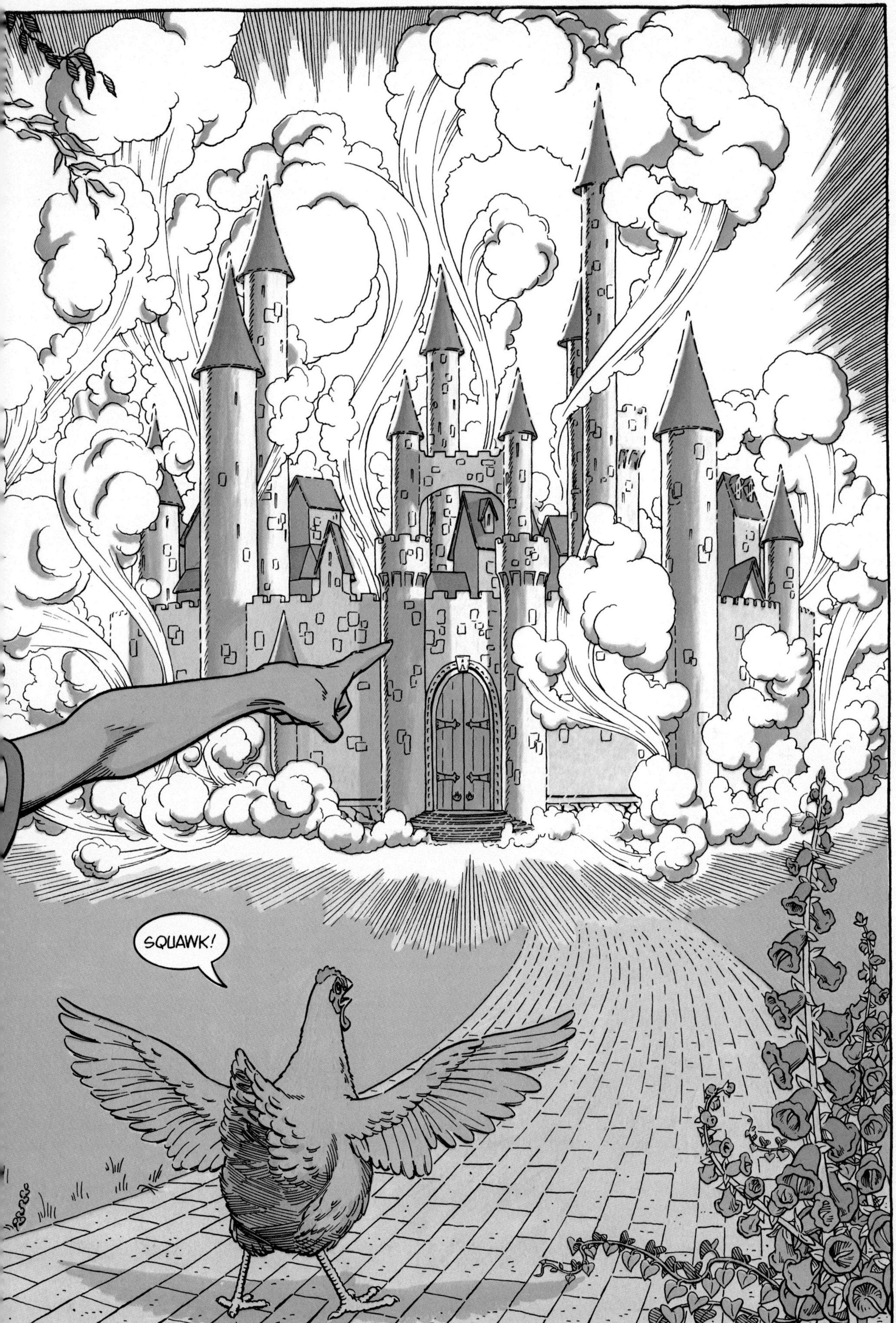
SQUAWK!

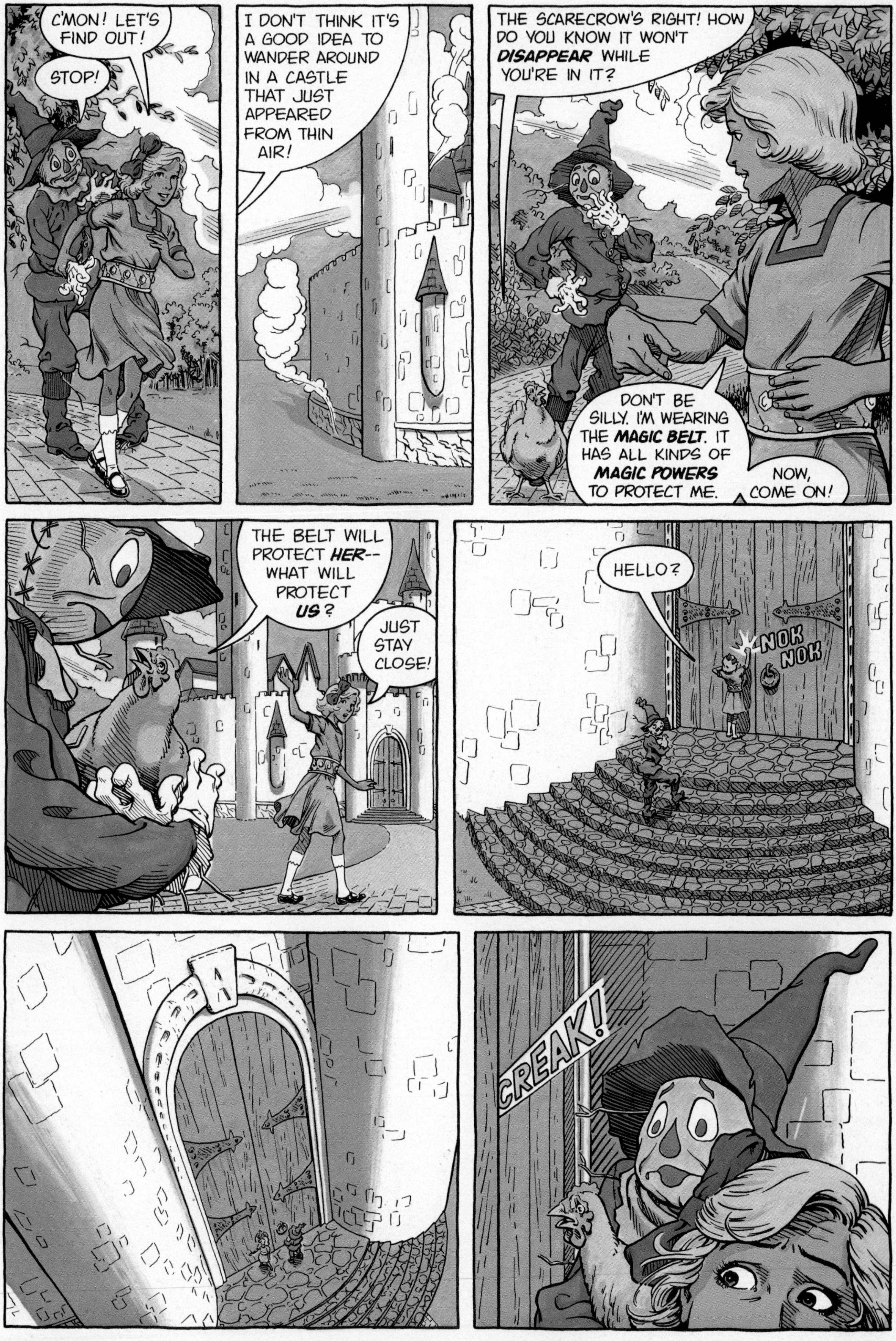

C'MON! LET'S FIND OUT!
STOP!
I DON'T THINK IT'S A GOOD IDEA TO WANDER AROUND IN A CASTLE THAT JUST APPEARED FROM THIN AIR!
THE SCARECROW'S RIGHT! HOW DO YOU KNOW IT WON'T **DISAPPEAR** WHILE YOU'RE IN IT?
DON'T BE SILLY. I'M WEARING THE **MAGIC BELT**. IT HAS ALL KINDS OF **MAGIC POWERS** TO PROTECT ME.
NOW, COME ON!
THE BELT WILL PROTECT **HER**-- WHAT WILL PROTECT **US**?
JUST STAY CLOSE!
HELLO?
NOK NOK
CREAK!

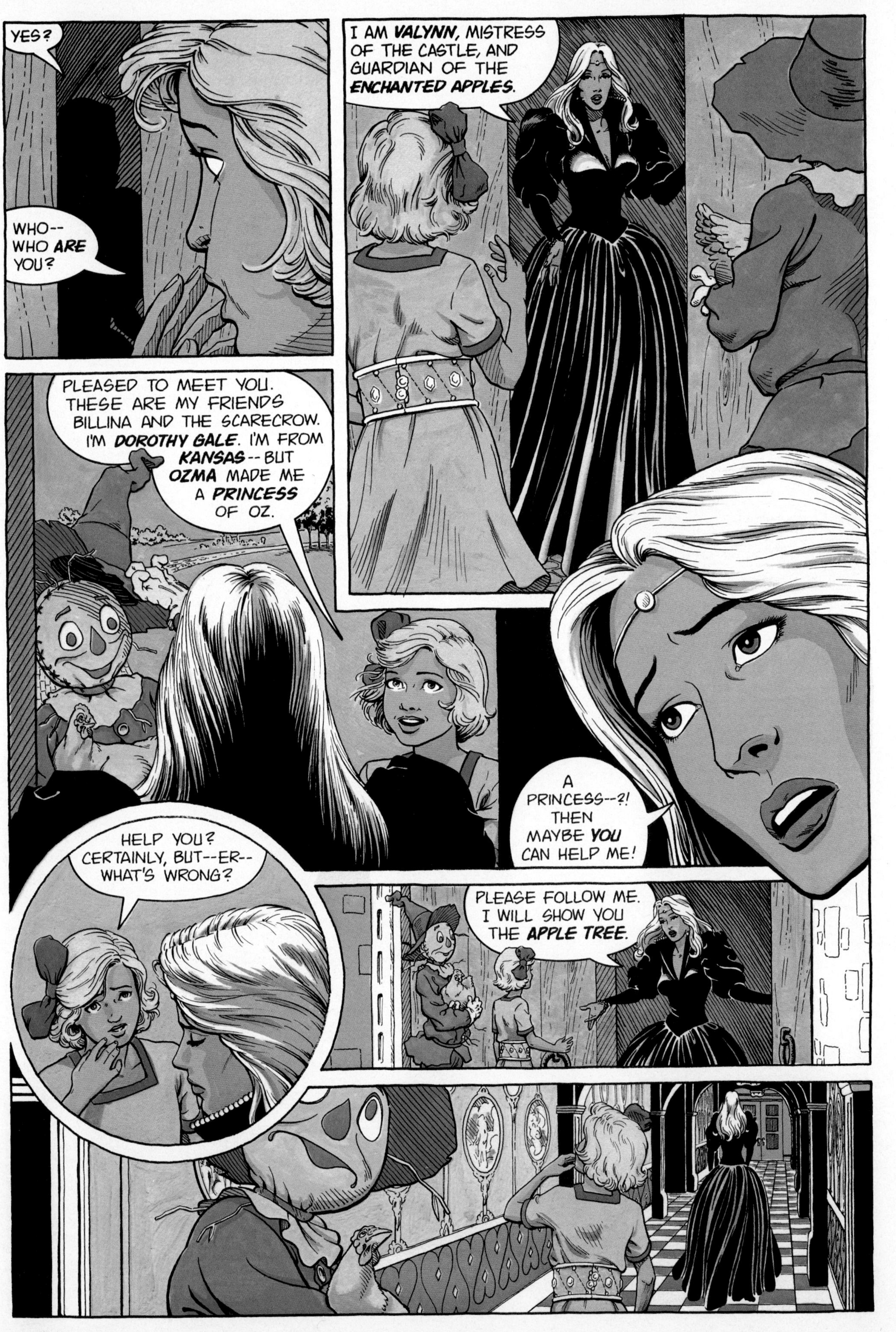
YES?
WHO-- WHO ARE YOU?
I AM VALYNN, MISTRESS OF THE CASTLE, AND GUARDIAN OF THE ENCHANTED APPLES.
PLEASED TO MEET YOU. THESE ARE MY FRIENDS BILLINA AND THE SCARECROW. I'M DOROTHY GALE. I'M FROM KANSAS--BUT OZMA MADE ME A PRINCESS OF OZ.
A PRINCESS--?! THEN MAYBE YOU CAN HELP ME!
HELP YOU? CERTAINLY, BUT--ER-- WHAT'S WRONG?
PLEASE FOLLOW ME. I WILL SHOW YOU THE APPLE TREE.

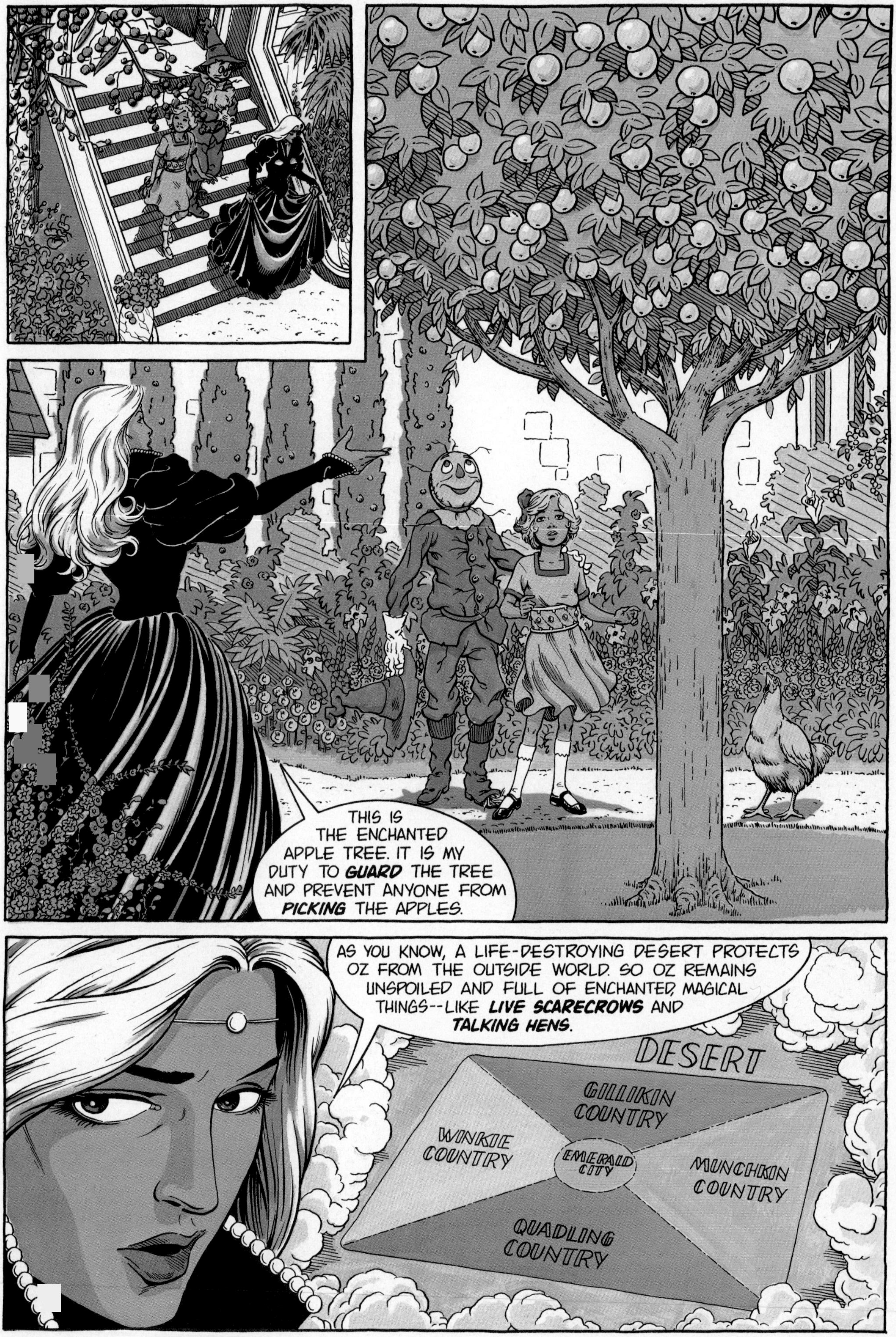
THIS IS THE ENCHANTED APPLE TREE. IT IS MY DUTY TO **GUARD** THE TREE AND PREVENT ANYONE FROM **PICKING** THE APPLES.
AS YOU KNOW, A LIFE-DESTROYING DESERT PROTECTS OZ FROM THE OUTSIDE WORLD. SO OZ REMAINS UNSPOILED AND FULL OF ENCHANTED, MAGICAL THINGS--LIKE **LIVE SCARECROWS** AND **TALKING HENS**.
DESERT
GILLIKIN COUNTRY
WINKIE COUNTRY
EMERALD CITY
MUNCHKIN COUNTRY
QUADLING COUNTRY

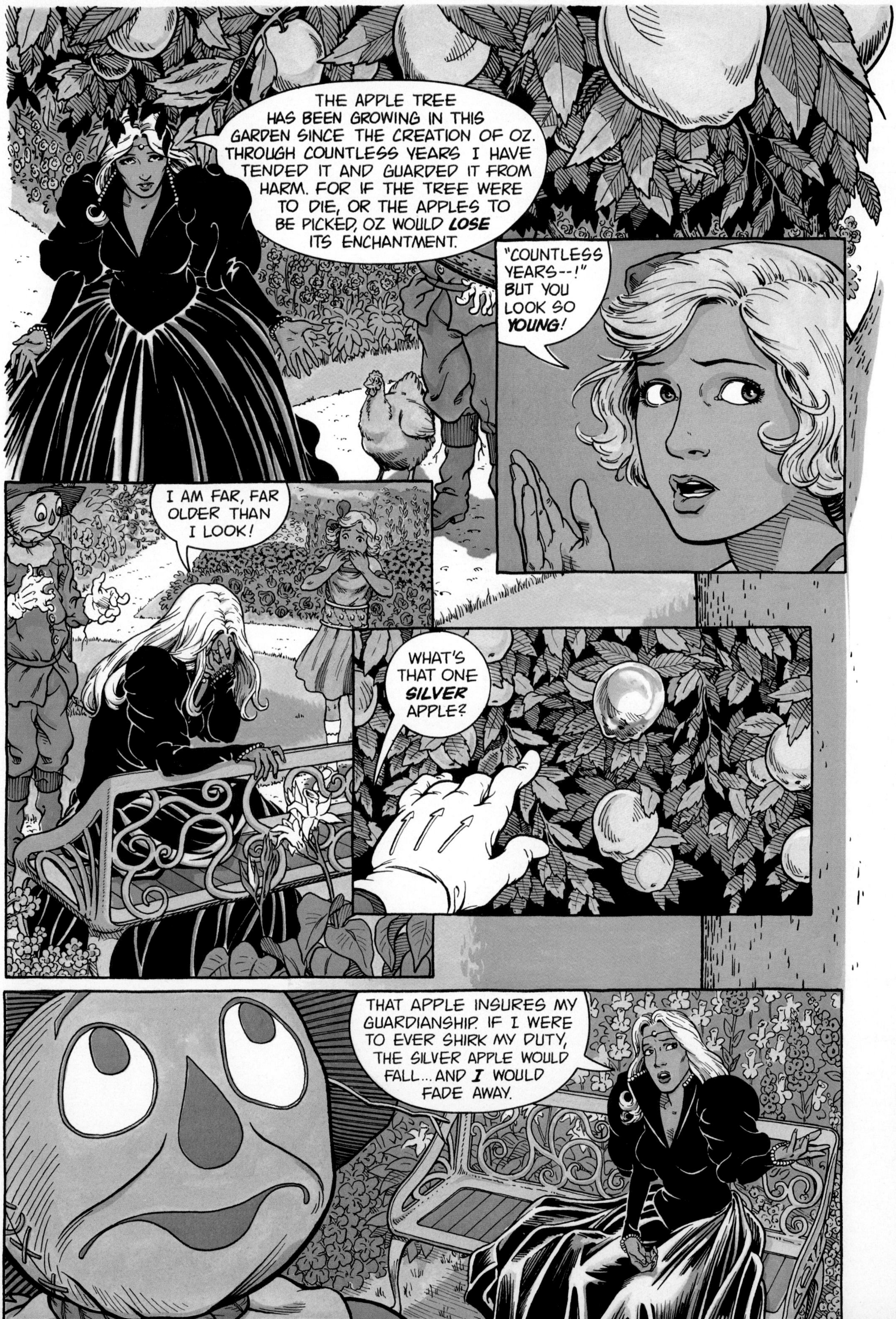
THE APPLE TREE HAS BEEN GROWING IN THIS GARDEN SINCE THE CREATION OF OZ. THROUGH COUNTLESS YEARS I HAVE TENDED IT AND GUARDED IT FROM HARM. FOR IF THE TREE WERE TO DIE, OR THE APPLES TO BE PICKED, OZ WOULD **LOSE** ITS ENCHANTMENT.
"COUNTLESS YEARS--!" BUT YOU LOOK SO ***YOUNG***!
I AM FAR, FAR OLDER THAN I LOOK!
WHAT'S THAT ONE ***SILVER*** APPLE?
THAT APPLE INSURES MY GUARDIANSHIP. IF I WERE TO EVER SHIRK MY DUTY, THE SILVER APPLE WOULD FALL... AND ***I*** WOULD FADE AWAY.

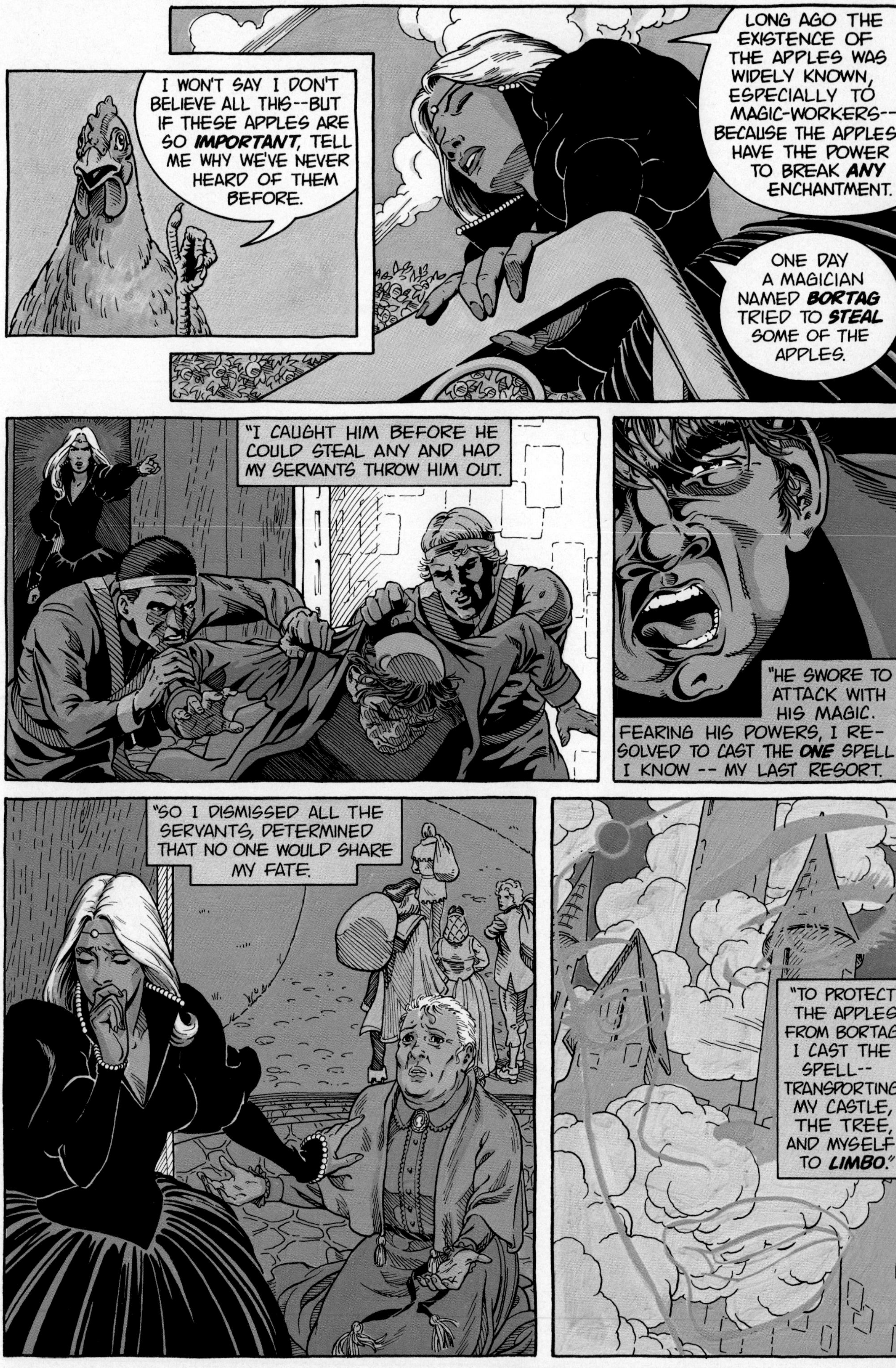
I WON'T SAY I DON'T BELIEVE ALL THIS--BUT IF THESE APPLES ARE SO IMPORTANT, TELL ME WHY WE'VE NEVER HEARD OF THEM BEFORE.
LONG AGO THE EXISTENCE OF THE APPLES WAS WIDELY KNOWN, ESPECIALLY TO MAGIC-WORKERS--BECAUSE THE APPLES HAVE THE POWER TO BREAK ANY ENCHANTMENT.
ONE DAY A MAGICIAN NAMED BORTAG TRIED TO STEAL SOME OF THE APPLES.
"I CAUGHT HIM BEFORE HE COULD STEAL ANY AND HAD MY SERVANTS THROW HIM OUT.
"HE SWORE TO ATTACK WITH HIS MAGIC. FEARING HIS POWERS, I RE-SOLVED TO CAST THE ONE SPELL I KNOW -- MY LAST RESORT.
"SO I DISMISSED ALL THE SERVANTS, DETERMINED THAT NO ONE WOULD SHARE MY FATE.
"TO PROTECT THE APPLES FROM BORTAG, I CAST THE SPELL--TRANSPORTING MY CASTLE, THE TREE, AND MYSELF TO LIMBO."

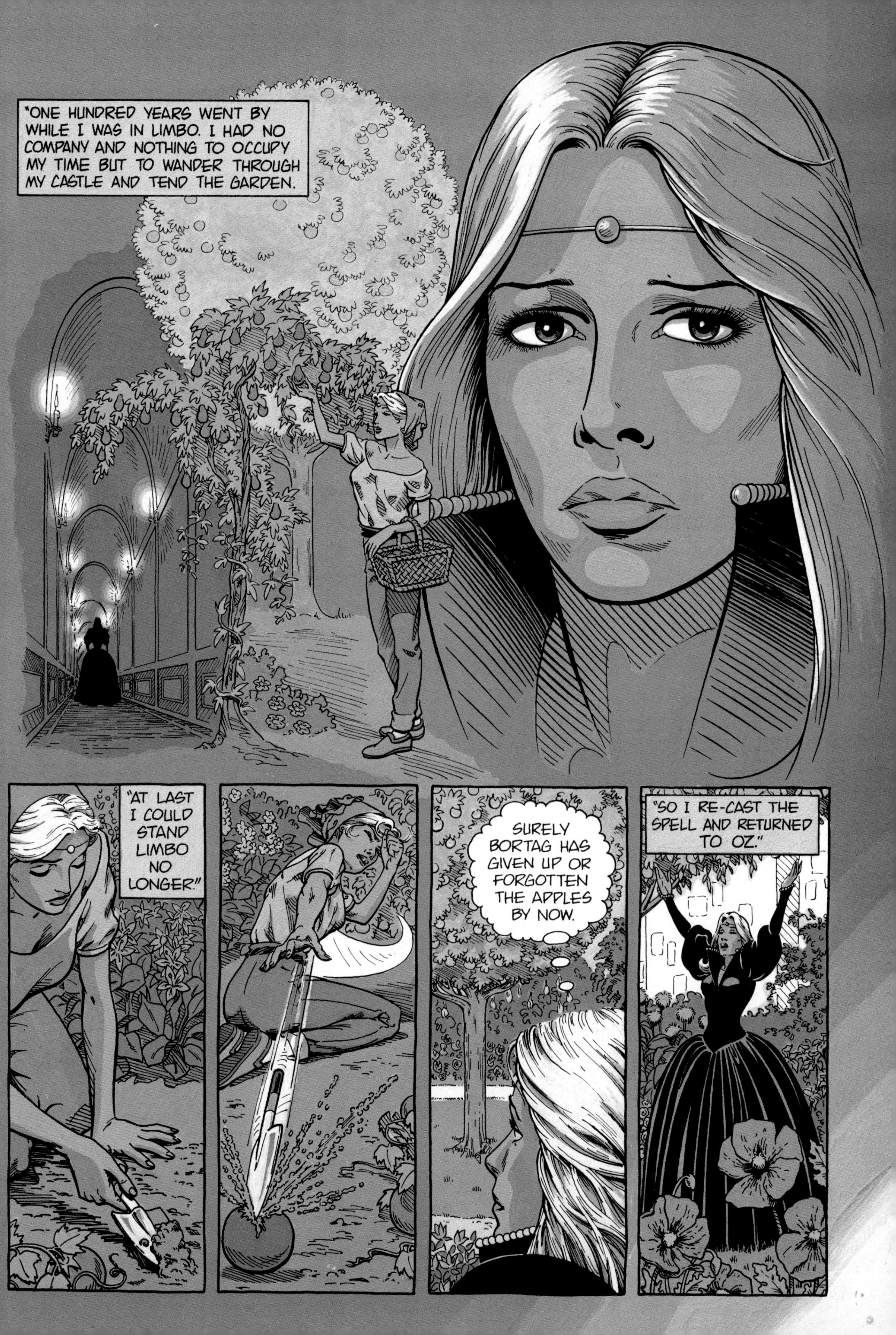
"ONE HUNDRED YEARS WENT BY WHILE I WAS IN LIMBO. I HAD NO COMPANY AND NOTHING TO OCCUPY MY TIME BUT TO WANDER THROUGH MY CASTLE AND TEND THE GARDEN.
"AT LAST I COULD STAND LIMBO NO LONGER."
SURELY BORTAG HAS GIVEN UP OR FORGOTTEN THE APPLES BY NOW.
"SO I RE-CAST THE SPELL AND RETURNED TO OZ."

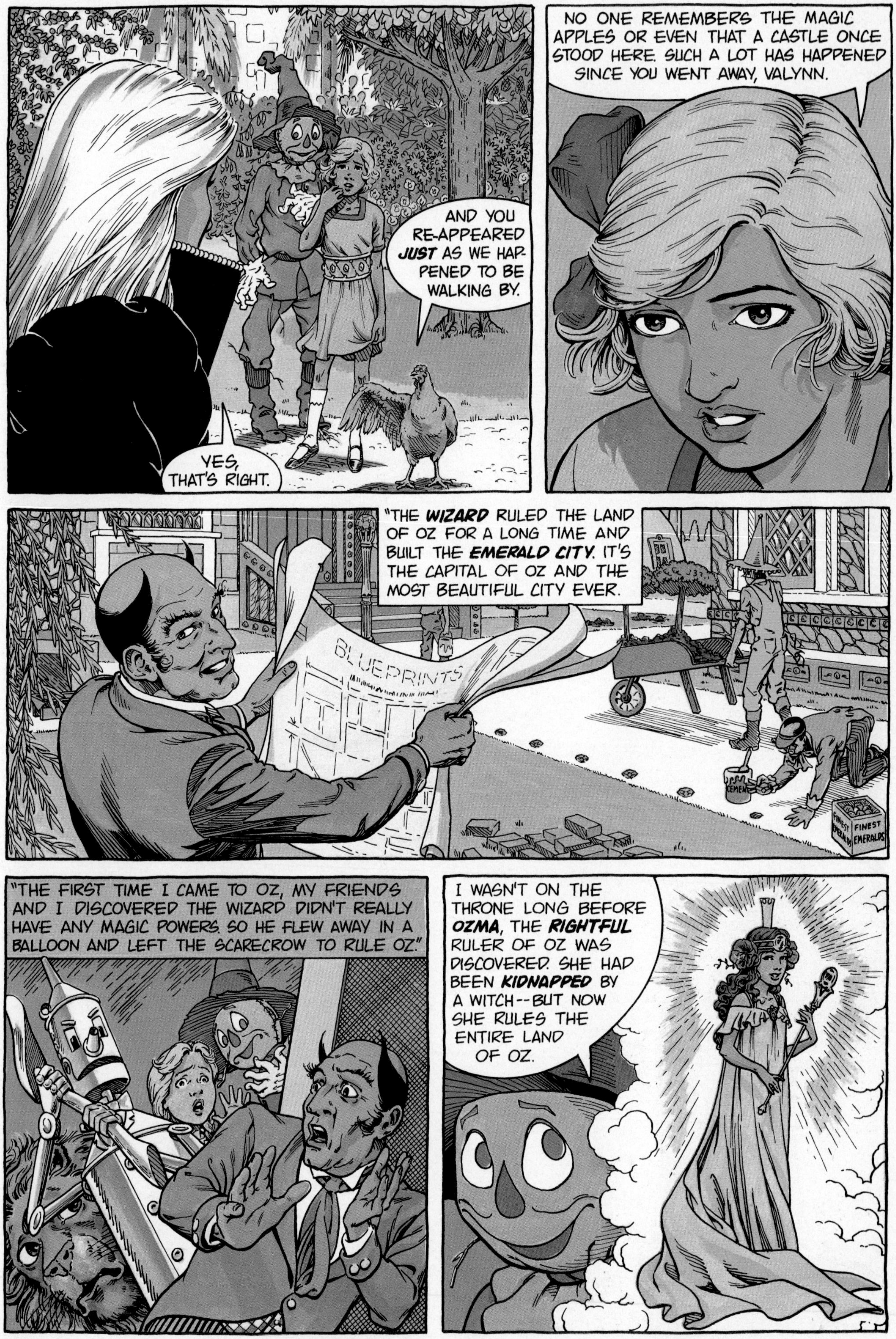
AND YOU RE-APPEARED JUST AS WE HAPPENED TO BE WALKING BY.
YES, THAT'S RIGHT.
NO ONE REMEMBERS THE MAGIC APPLES OR EVEN THAT A CASTLE ONCE STOOD HERE. SUCH A LOT HAS HAPPENED SINCE YOU WENT AWAY, VALYNN.
"THE WIZARD RULED THE LAND OF OZ FOR A LONG TIME AND BUILT THE EMERALD CITY. IT'S THE CAPITAL OF OZ AND THE MOST BEAUTIFUL CITY EVER.
BLUEPRINTS
CEMENT
FINEST EMERALDS
FINEST EMERALDS
"THE FIRST TIME I CAME TO OZ, MY FRIENDS AND I DISCOVERED THE WIZARD DIDN'T REALLY HAVE ANY MAGIC POWERS. SO HE FLEW AWAY IN A BALLOON AND LEFT THE SCARECROW TO RULE OZ."
I WASN'T ON THE THRONE LONG BEFORE OZMA, THE RIGHTFUL RULER OF OZ WAS DISCOVERED. SHE HAD BEEN KIDNAPPED BY A WITCH--BUT NOW SHE RULES THE ENTIRE LAND OF OZ.

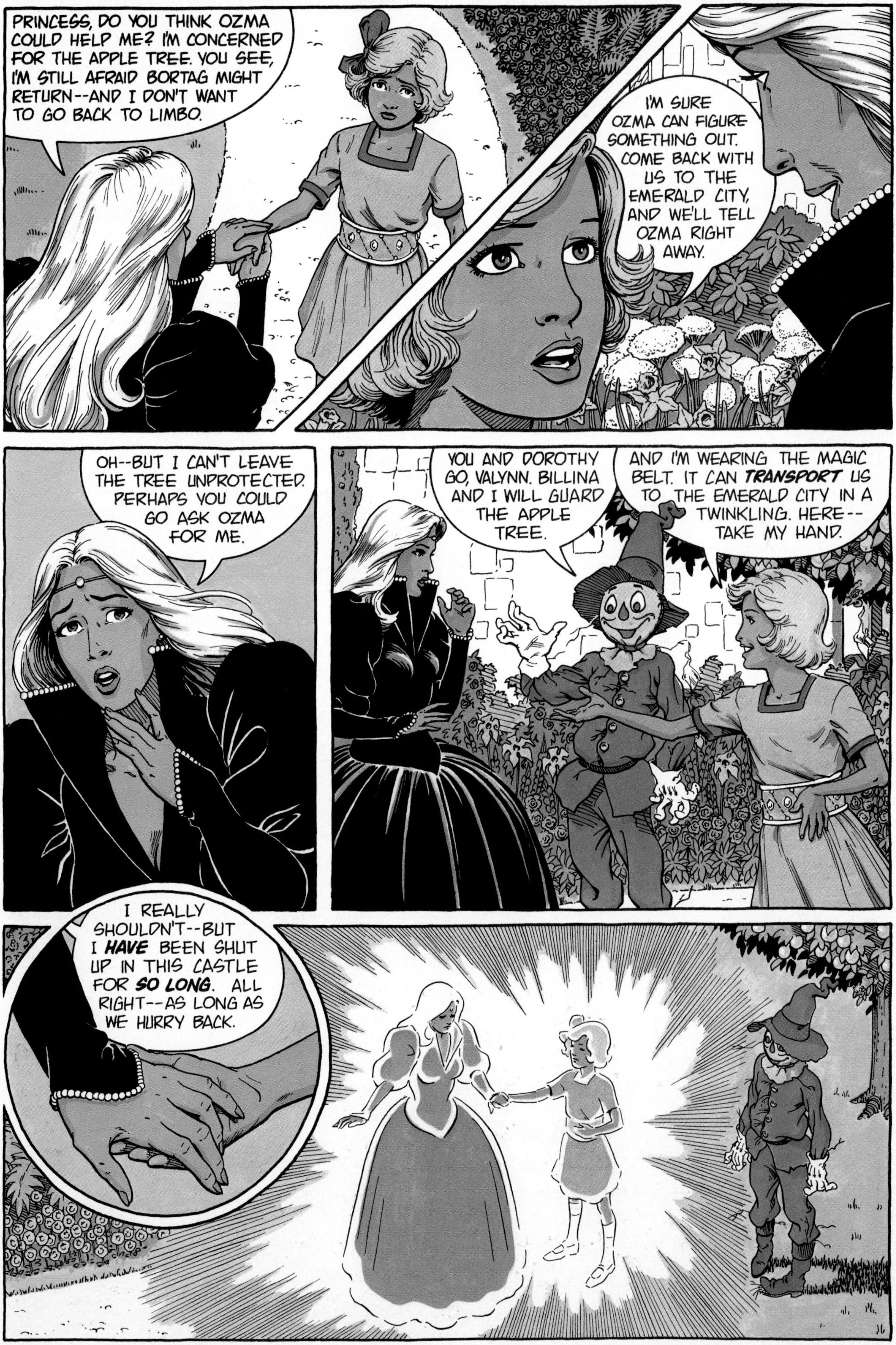
PRINCESS, DO YOU THINK OZMA COULD HELP ME? I'M CONCERNED FOR THE APPLE TREE. YOU SEE, I'M STILL AFRAID BORTAG MIGHT RETURN--AND I DON'T WANT TO GO BACK TO LIMBO.
I'M SURE OZMA CAN FIGURE SOMETHING OUT. COME BACK WITH US TO THE EMERALD CITY, AND WE'LL TELL OZMA RIGHT AWAY.
OH--BUT I CAN'T LEAVE THE TREE UNPROTECTED. PERHAPS YOU COULD GO ASK OZMA FOR ME.
YOU AND DOROTHY GO, VALYNN. BILLINA AND I WILL GUARD THE APPLE TREE.
AND I'M WEARING THE MAGIC BELT. IT CAN TRANSPORT US TO THE EMERALD CITY IN A TWINKLING. HERE--TAKE MY HAND.
I REALLY SHOULDN'T--BUT I HAVE BEEN SHUT UP IN THIS CASTLE FOR SO LONG. ALL RIGHT--AS LONG AS WE HURRY BACK.

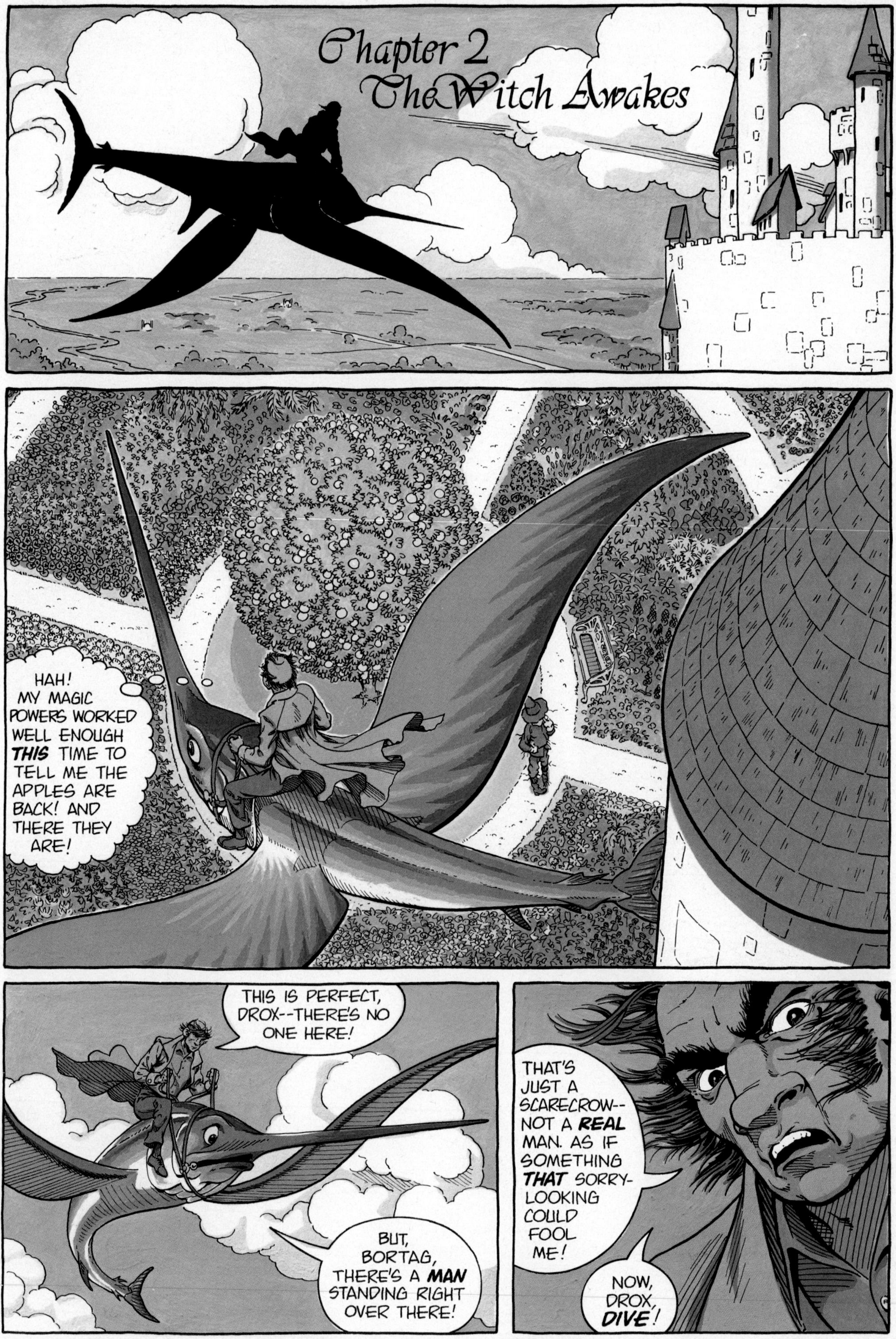
Chapter 2
The Witch Awakes
HAH! MY MAGIC POWERS WORKED WELL ENOUGH THIS TIME TO TELL ME THE APPLES ARE BACK! AND THERE THEY ARE!
THIS IS PERFECT, DROX--THERE'S NO ONE HERE!
BUT, BORTAG, THERE'S A MAN STANDING RIGHT OVER THERE!
THAT'S JUST A SCARECROW-- NOT A REAL MAN. AS IF SOMETHING THAT SORRY-LOOKING COULD FOOL ME!
NOW, DROX, DIVE!

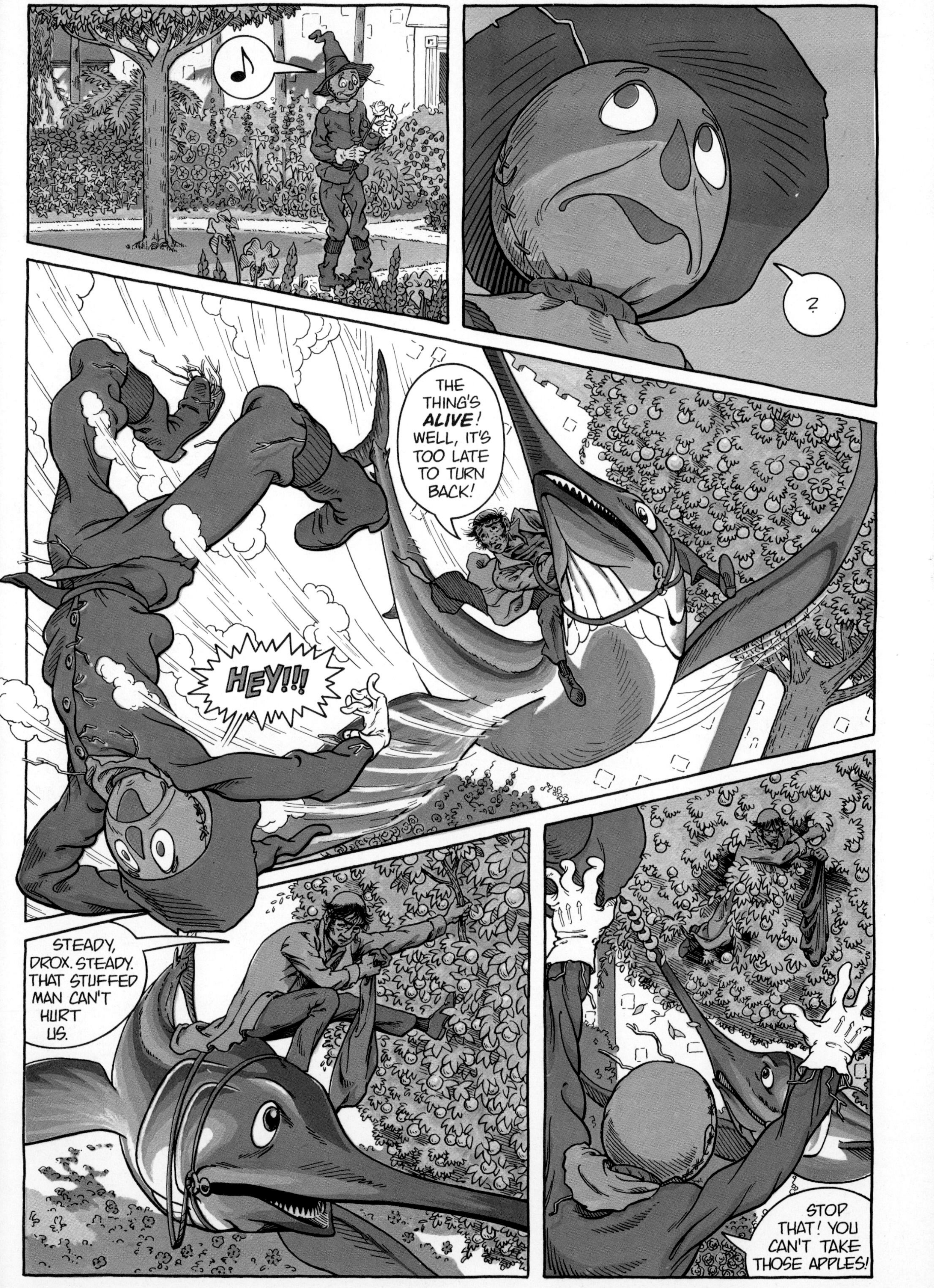
♪
?
THE THING'S ALIVE! WELL, IT'S TOO LATE TO TURN BACK!
HEY!!!
STEADY, DROX. STEADY. THAT STUFFED MAN CAN'T HURT US.
STOP THAT! YOU CAN'T TAKE THOSE APPLES!

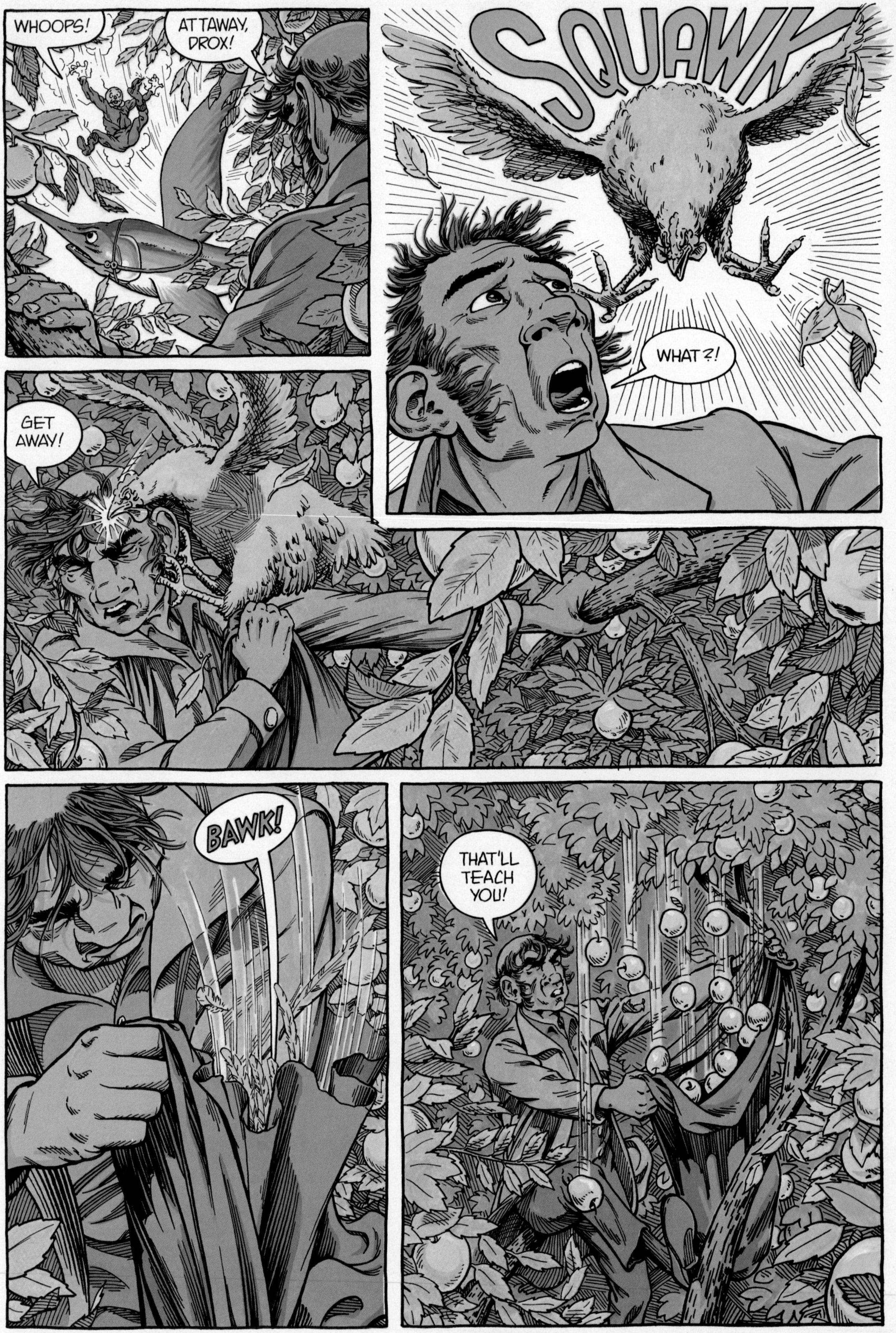
WHOOPS!
ATTAWAY, DROX!
SQUAWK
WHAT?!
GET AWAY!
BAWK!
THAT'LL TEACH YOU!

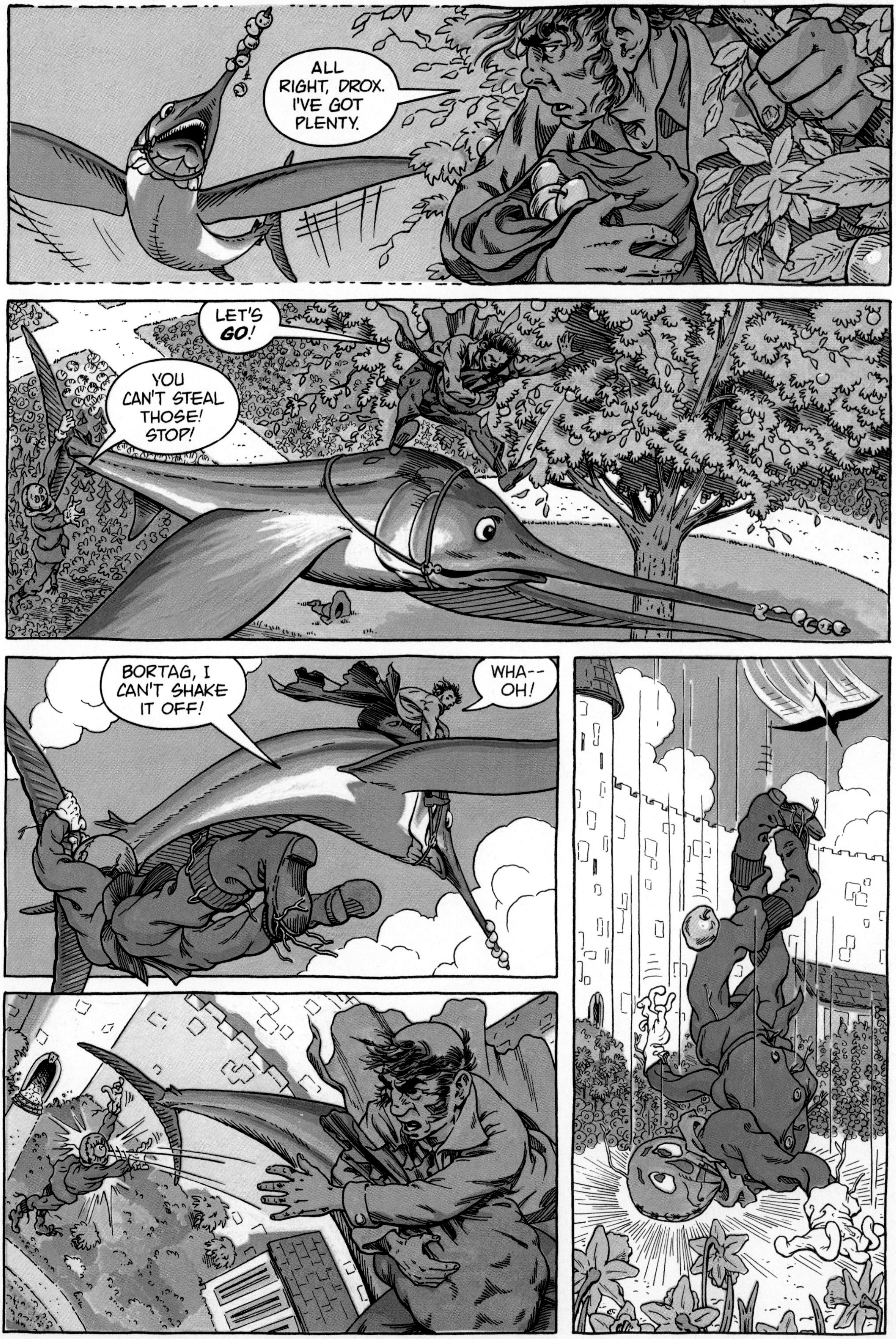
ALL RIGHT, DROX. I'VE GOT PLENTY.
LET'S GO!
YOU CAN'T STEAL THOSE! STOP!
BORTAG, I CAN'T SHAKE IT OFF!
WHA-- OH!

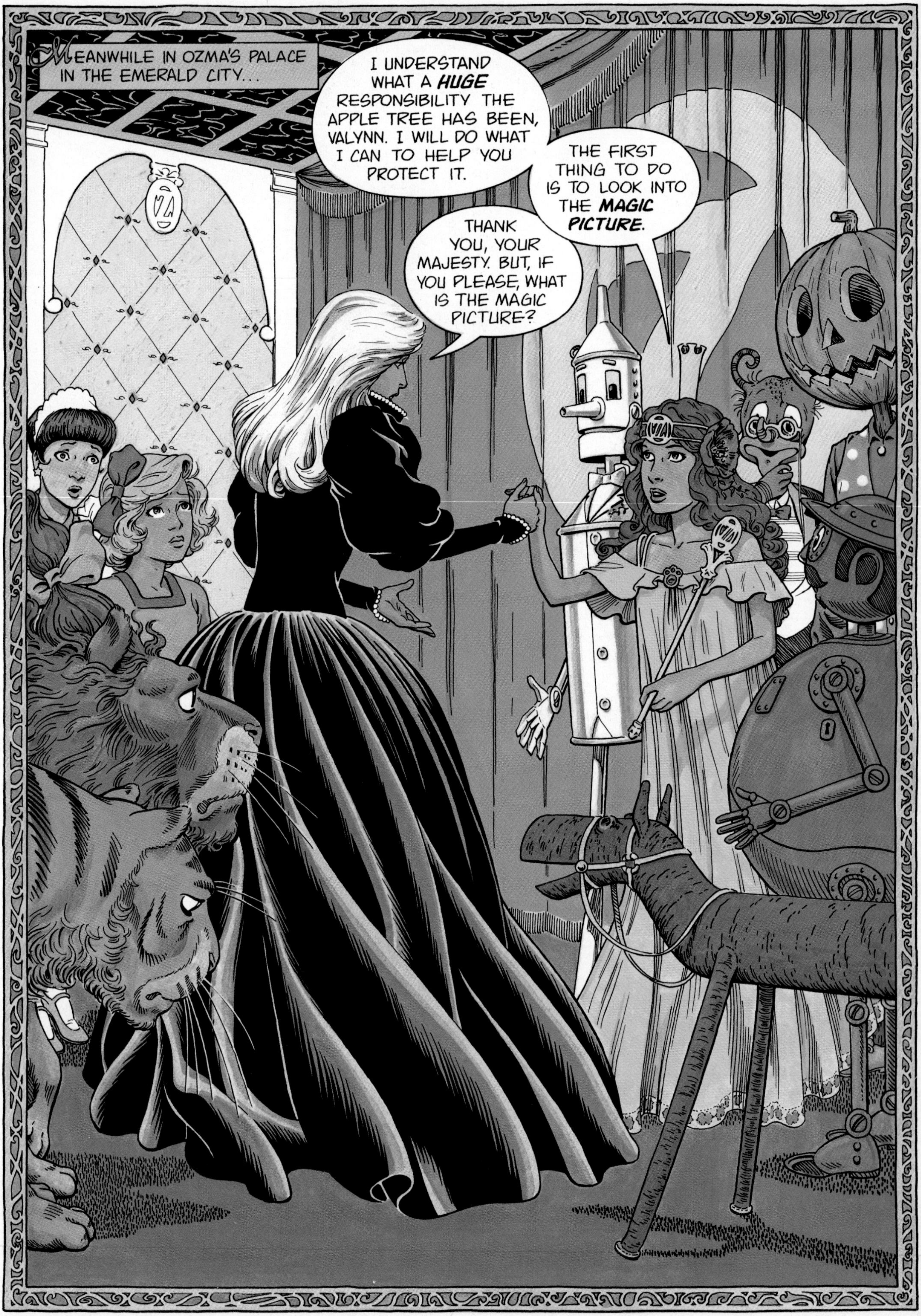
MEANWHILE IN OZMA'S PALACE IN THE EMERALD CITY...
I UNDERSTAND WHAT A HUGE RESPONSIBILITY THE APPLE TREE HAS BEEN, VALYNN. I WILL DO WHAT I CAN TO HELP YOU PROTECT IT.
THE FIRST THING TO DO IS TO LOOK INTO THE MAGIC PICTURE.
THANK YOU, YOUR MAJESTY. BUT, IF YOU PLEASE, WHAT IS THE MAGIC PICTURE?

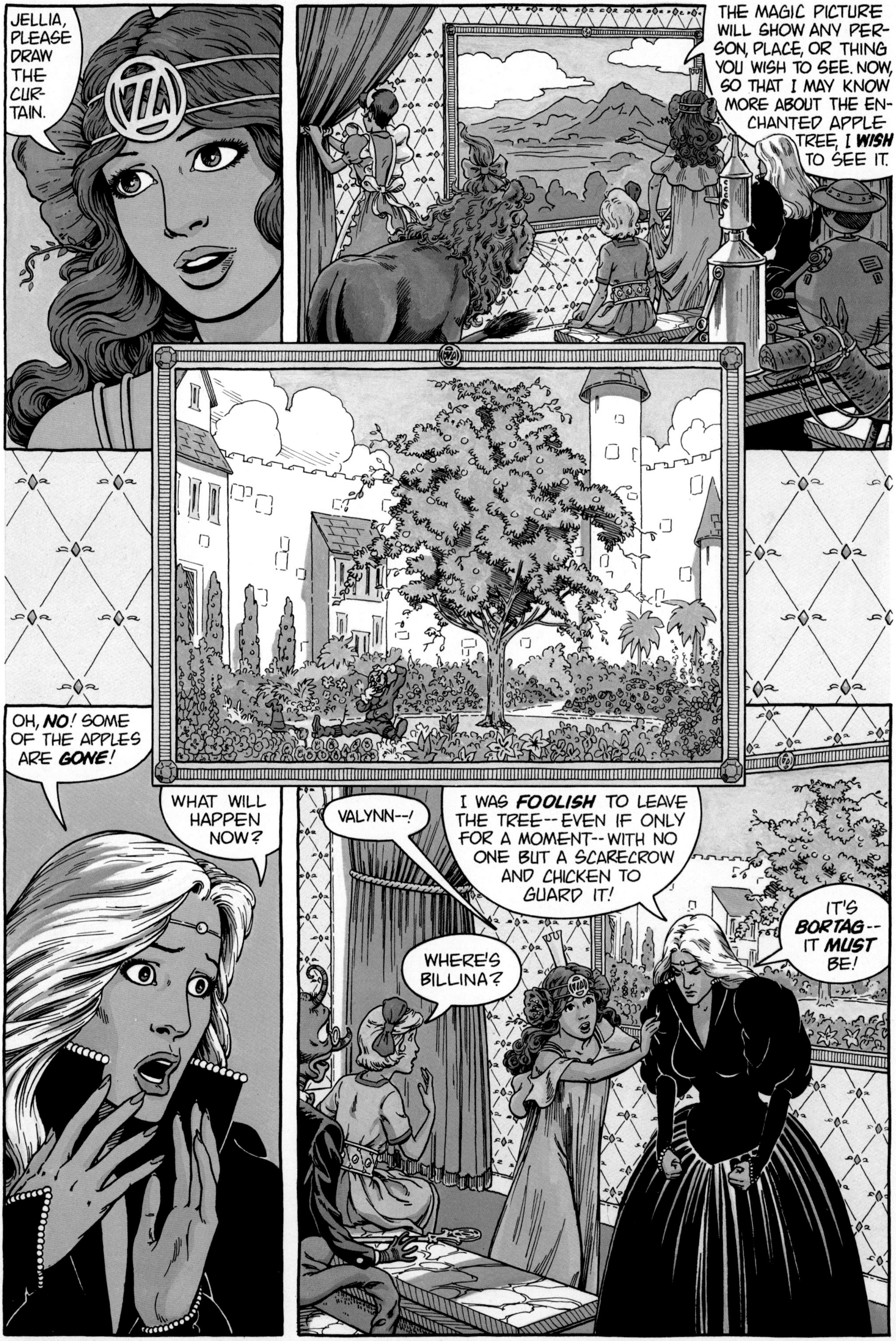
JELLIA, PLEASE DRAW THE CURTAIN.
THE MAGIC PICTURE WILL SHOW ANY PERSON, PLACE, OR THING YOU WISH TO SEE. NOW, SO THAT I MAY KNOW MORE ABOUT THE ENCHANTED APPLE TREE, I **WISH** TO SEE IT.
OH, **NO**! SOME OF THE APPLES ARE **GONE**!
WHAT WILL HAPPEN NOW?
VALYNN--!
I WAS **FOOLISH** TO LEAVE THE TREE--EVEN IF ONLY FOR A MOMENT--WITH NO ONE BUT A SCARECROW AND CHICKEN TO GUARD IT!
IT'S **BORTAG**--IT **MUST** BE!
WHERE'S BILLINA?

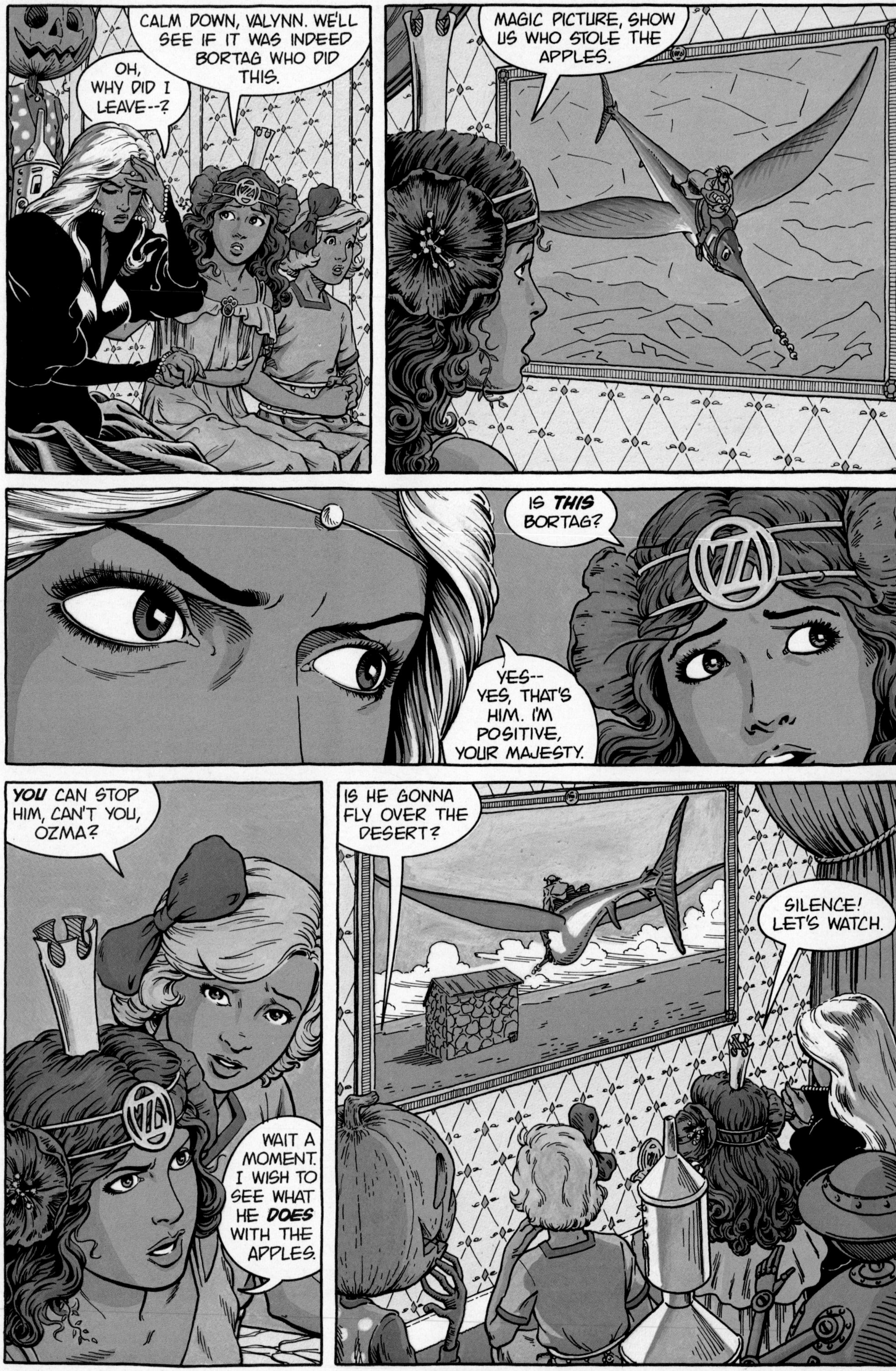
CALM DOWN, VALYNN. WE'LL SEE IF IT WAS INDEED BORTAG WHO DID THIS.
OH, WHY DID I LEAVE--?
MAGIC PICTURE, SHOW US WHO STOLE THE APPLES.
IS **THIS** BORTAG?
YES-- YES, THAT'S HIM. I'M POSITIVE, YOUR MAJESTY.
YOU CAN STOP HIM, CAN'T YOU, OZMA?
WAIT A MOMENT. I WISH TO SEE WHAT HE **DOES** WITH THE APPLES.
IS HE GONNA FLY OVER THE DESERT?
SILENCE! LET'S WATCH.

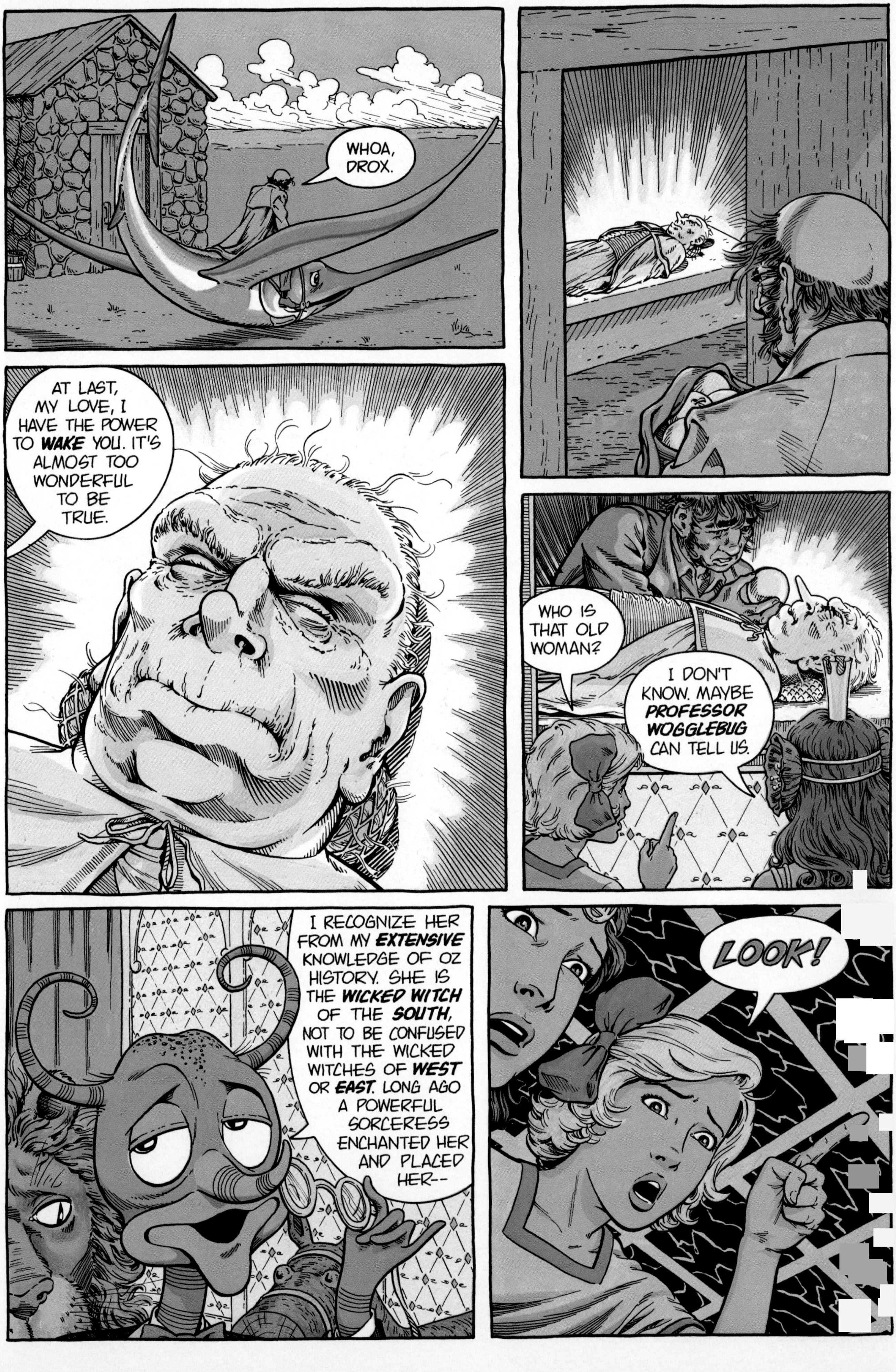
WHOA, DROX.
AT LAST, MY LOVE, I HAVE THE POWER TO **WAKE** YOU. IT'S ALMOST TOO WONDERFUL TO BE TRUE.
WHO IS THAT OLD WOMAN?
I DON'T KNOW. MAYBE **PROFESSOR WOGGLEBUG** CAN TELL US.
I RECOGNIZE HER FROM MY **EXTENSIVE** KNOWLEDGE OF OZ HISTORY. SHE IS THE **WICKED WITCH** OF THE **SOUTH**, NOT TO BE CONFUSED WITH THE WICKED WITCHES OF **WEST** OR **EAST**. LONG AGO A POWERFUL SORCERESS ENCHANTED HER AND PLACED HER--
LOOK!

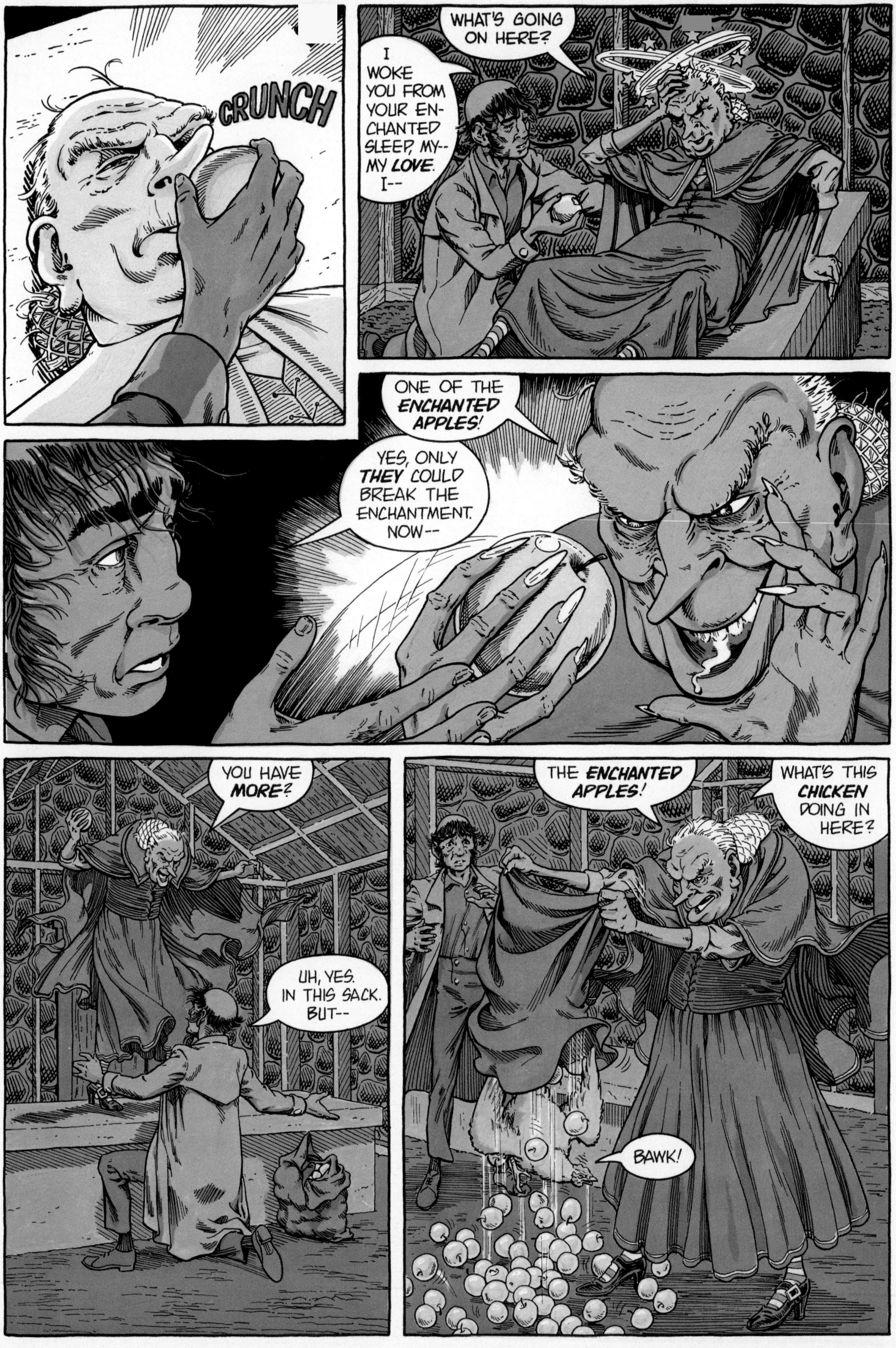
CRUNCH
WHAT'S GOING ON HERE?
I WOKE YOU FROM YOUR EN-CHANTED SLEEP, MY-- MY LOVE. I--
ONE OF THE ENCHANTED APPLES!
YES, ONLY THEY COULD BREAK THE ENCHANTMENT. NOW--
YOU HAVE MORE?
UH, YES. IN THIS SACK. BUT--
THE ENCHANTED APPLES!
WHAT'S THIS CHICKEN DOING IN HERE?
BAWK!

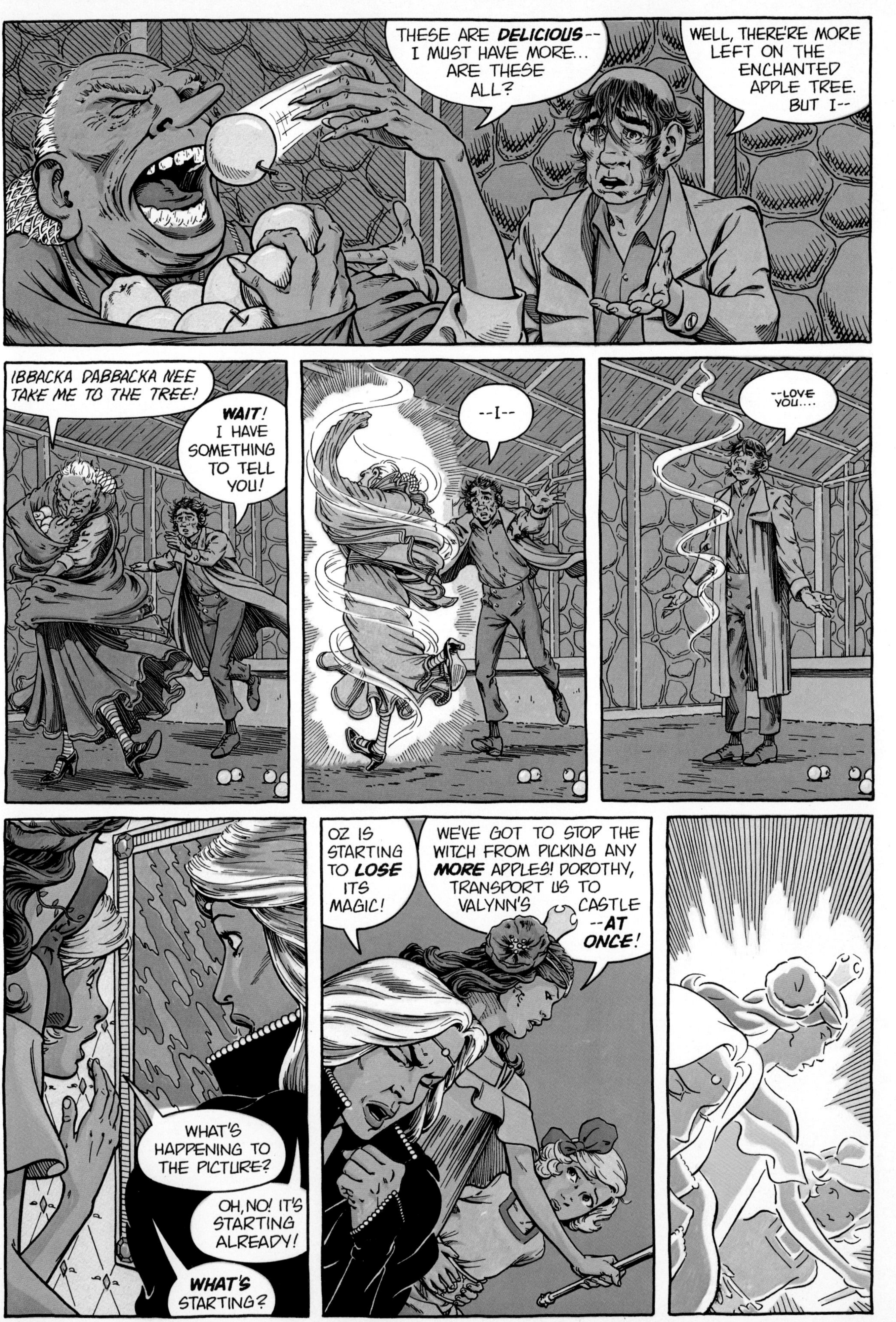
THESE ARE DELICIOUS-- I MUST HAVE MORE... ARE THESE ALL?
WELL, THERE'RE MORE LEFT ON THE ENCHANTED APPLE TREE. BUT I--
IBBACKA DABBACKA NEE TAKE ME TO THE TREE!
WAIT! I HAVE SOMETHING TO TELL YOU!
--I--
--LOVE YOU....
WHAT'S HAPPENING TO THE PICTURE?
OH, NO! IT'S STARTING ALREADY!
WHAT'S STARTING?
OZ IS STARTING TO LOSE ITS MAGIC!
WE'VE GOT TO STOP THE WITCH FROM PICKING ANY MORE APPLES! DOROTHY, TRANSPORT US TO VALYNN'S CASTLE --AT ONCE!

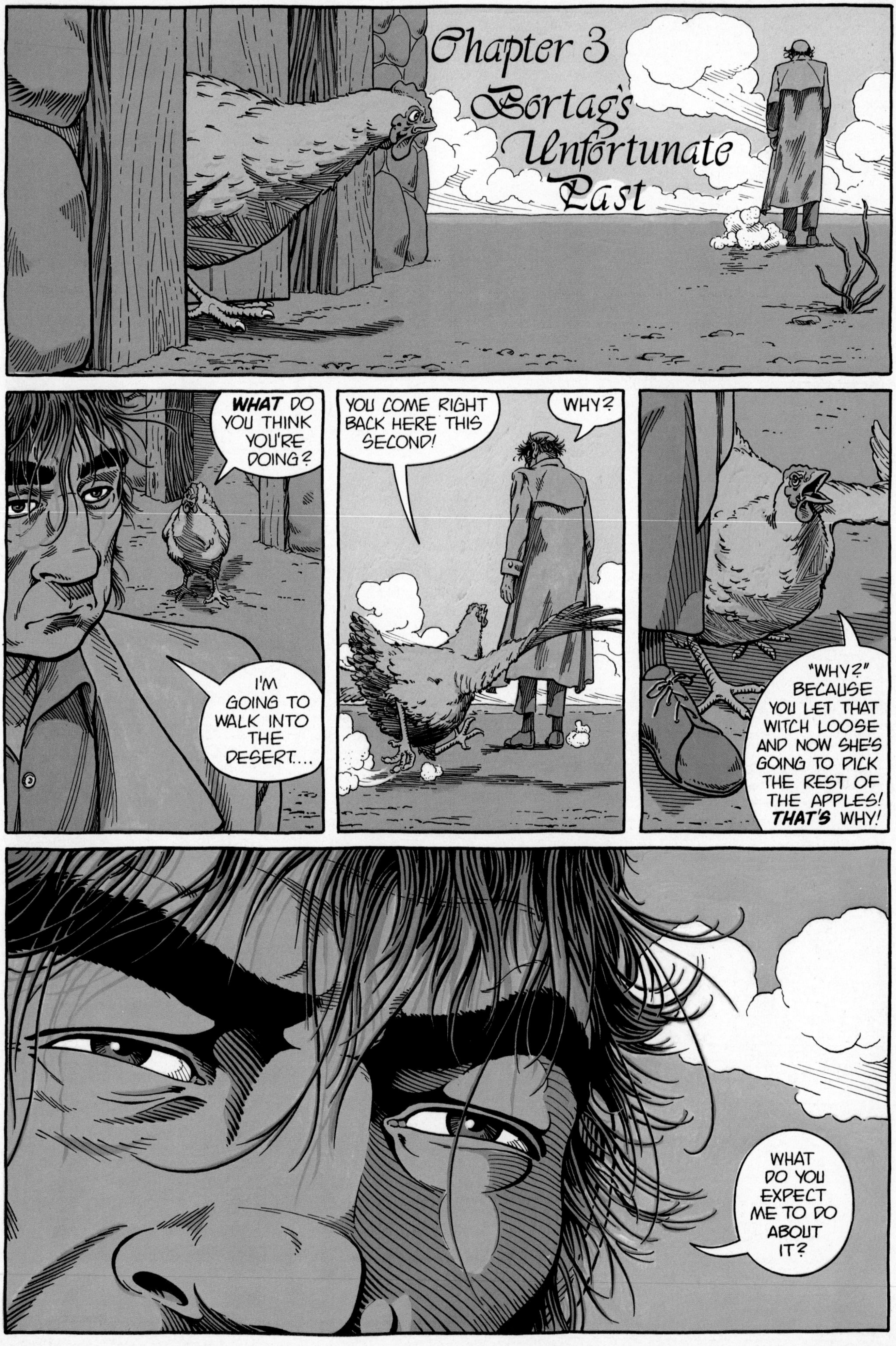
Chapter 3
Bortag's Unfortunate Past
WHAT DO YOU THINK YOU'RE DOING?
I'M GOING TO WALK INTO THE DESERT....
YOU COME RIGHT BACK HERE THIS SECOND!
WHY?
"WHY?" BECAUSE YOU LET THAT WITCH LOOSE AND NOW SHE'S GOING TO PICK THE REST OF THE APPLES! THAT'S WHY!
WHAT DO YOU EXPECT ME TO DO ABOUT IT?

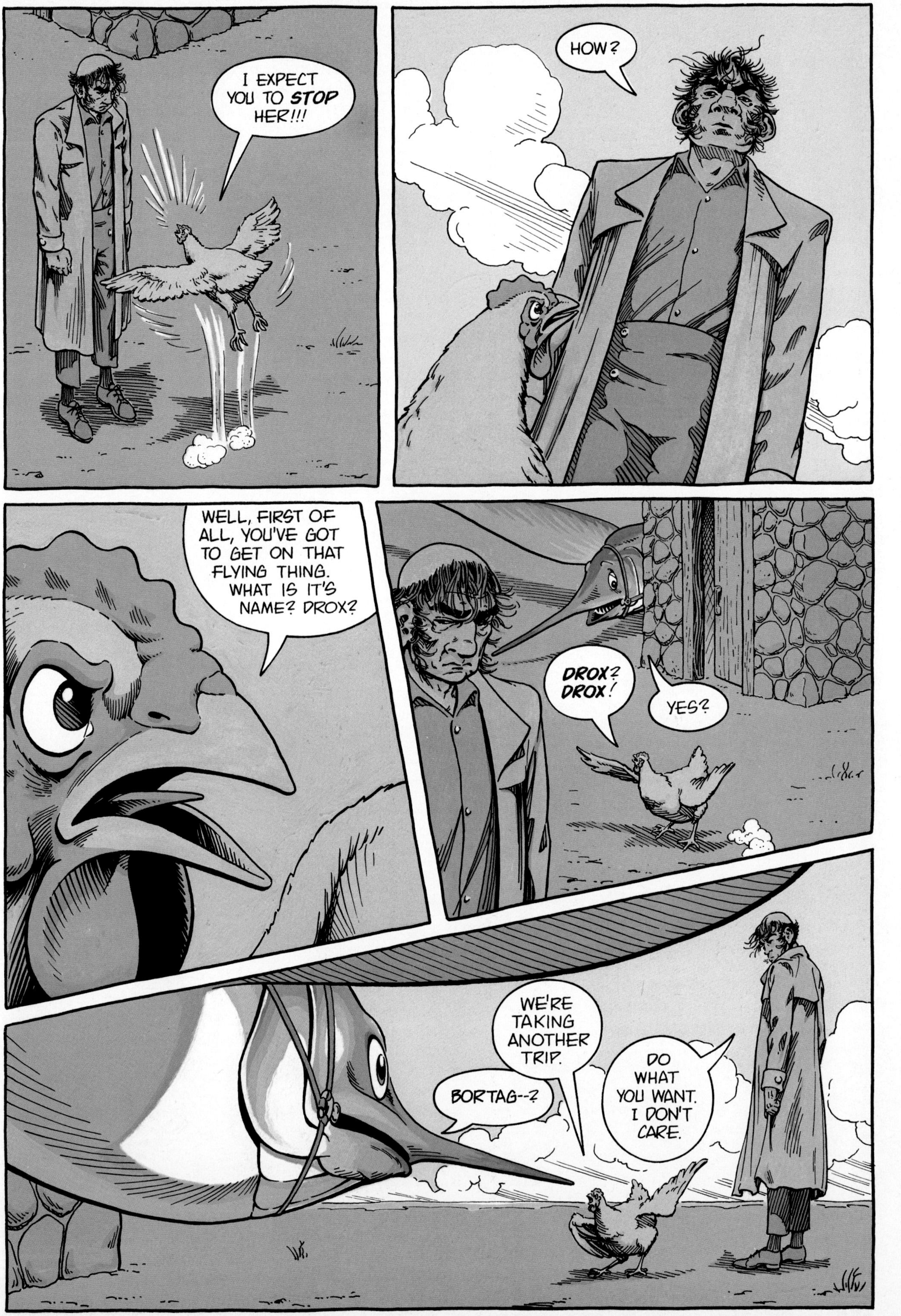
I EXPECT YOU TO **STOP** HER!!!
HOW?
WELL, FIRST OF ALL, YOU'VE GOT TO GET ON THAT FLYING THING. WHAT IS IT'S NAME? DROX?
DROX? DROX!
YES?
WE'RE TAKING ANOTHER TRIP.
BORTAG--?
DO WHAT YOU WANT. I DON'T CARE.

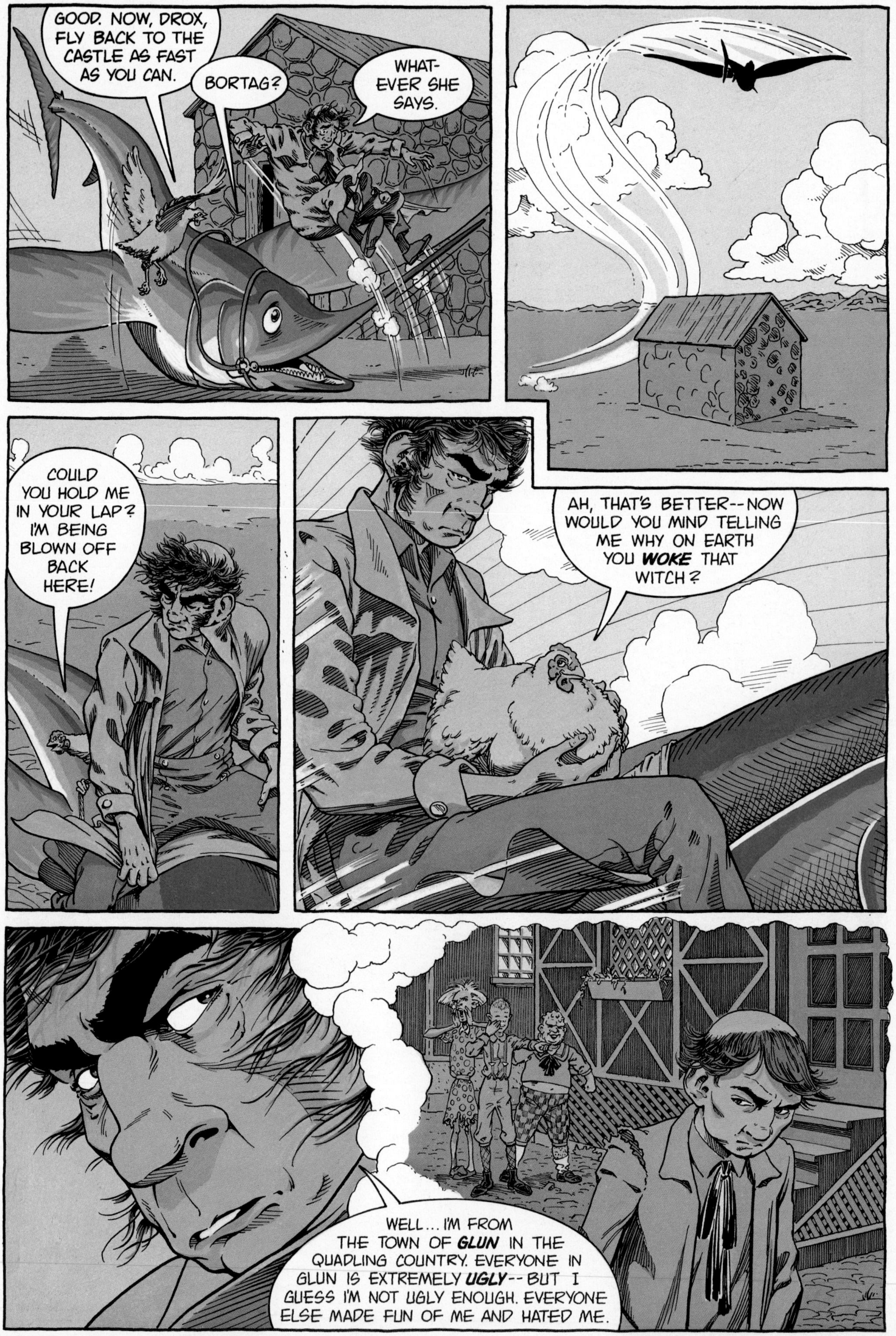
GOOD. NOW, DROX, FLY BACK TO THE CASTLE AS FAST AS YOU CAN.
BORTAG?
WHAT-EVER SHE SAYS.
COULD YOU HOLD ME IN YOUR LAP? I'M BEING BLOWN OFF BACK HERE!
AH, THAT'S BETTER--NOW WOULD YOU MIND TELLING ME WHY ON EARTH YOU WOKE THAT WITCH?
WELL... I'M FROM THE TOWN OF GLUN IN THE QUADLING COUNTRY. EVERYONE IN GLUN IS EXTREMELY UGLY--BUT I GUESS I'M NOT UGLY ENOUGH. EVERYONE ELSE MADE FUN OF ME AND HATED ME.

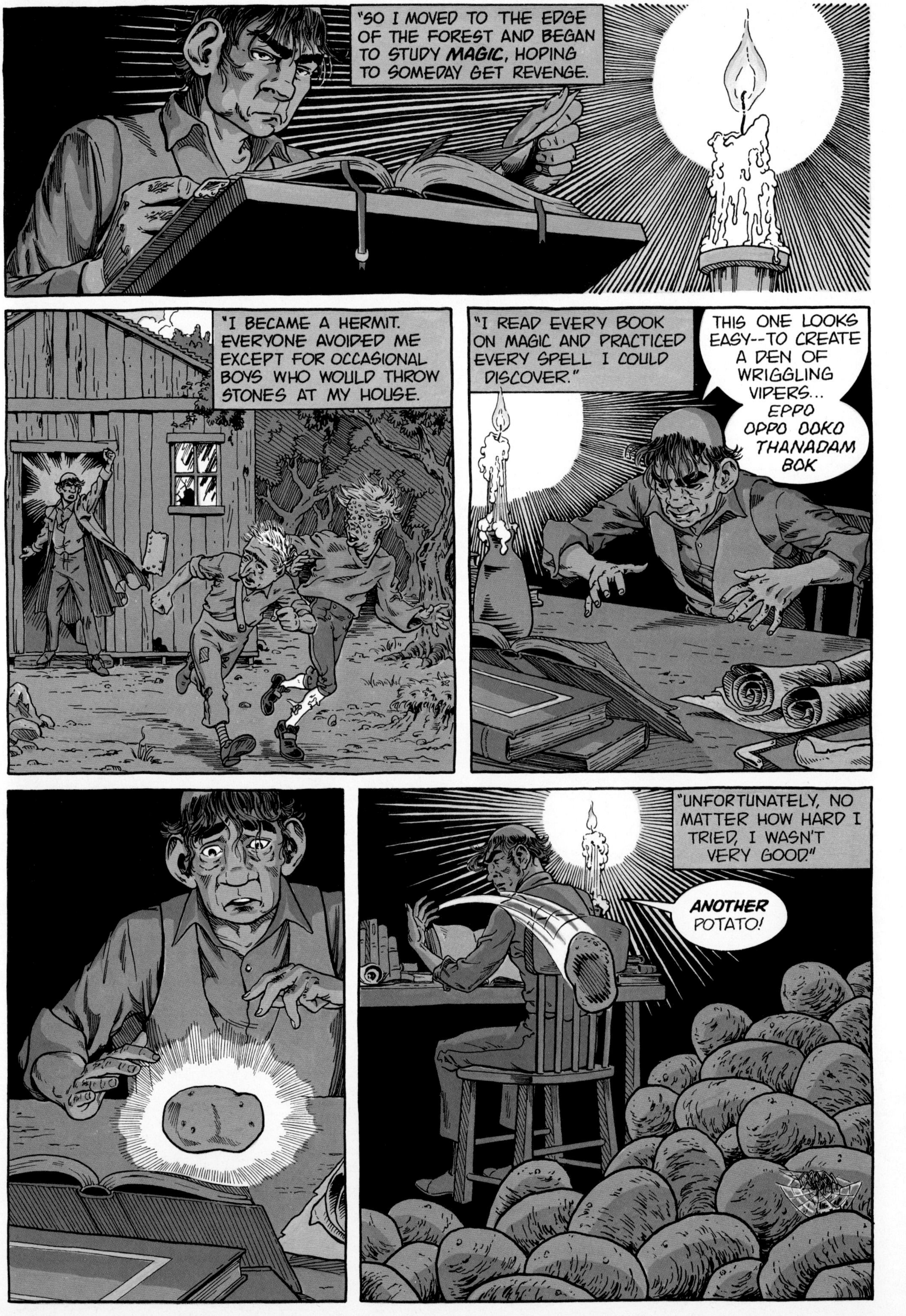
"SO I MOVED TO THE EDGE OF THE FOREST AND BEGAN TO STUDY MAGIC, HOPING TO SOMEDAY GET REVENGE.
"I BECAME A HERMIT. EVERYONE AVOIDED ME EXCEPT FOR OCCASIONAL BOYS WHO WOULD THROW STONES AT MY HOUSE.
"I READ EVERY BOOK ON MAGIC AND PRACTICED EVERY SPELL I COULD DISCOVER."
THIS ONE LOOKS EASY--TO CREATE A DEN OF WRIGGLING VIPERS... EPPO OPPO OOKO THANADAM BOK
"UNFORTUNATELY, NO MATTER HOW HARD I TRIED, I WASN'T VERY GOOD."
ANOTHER POTATO!

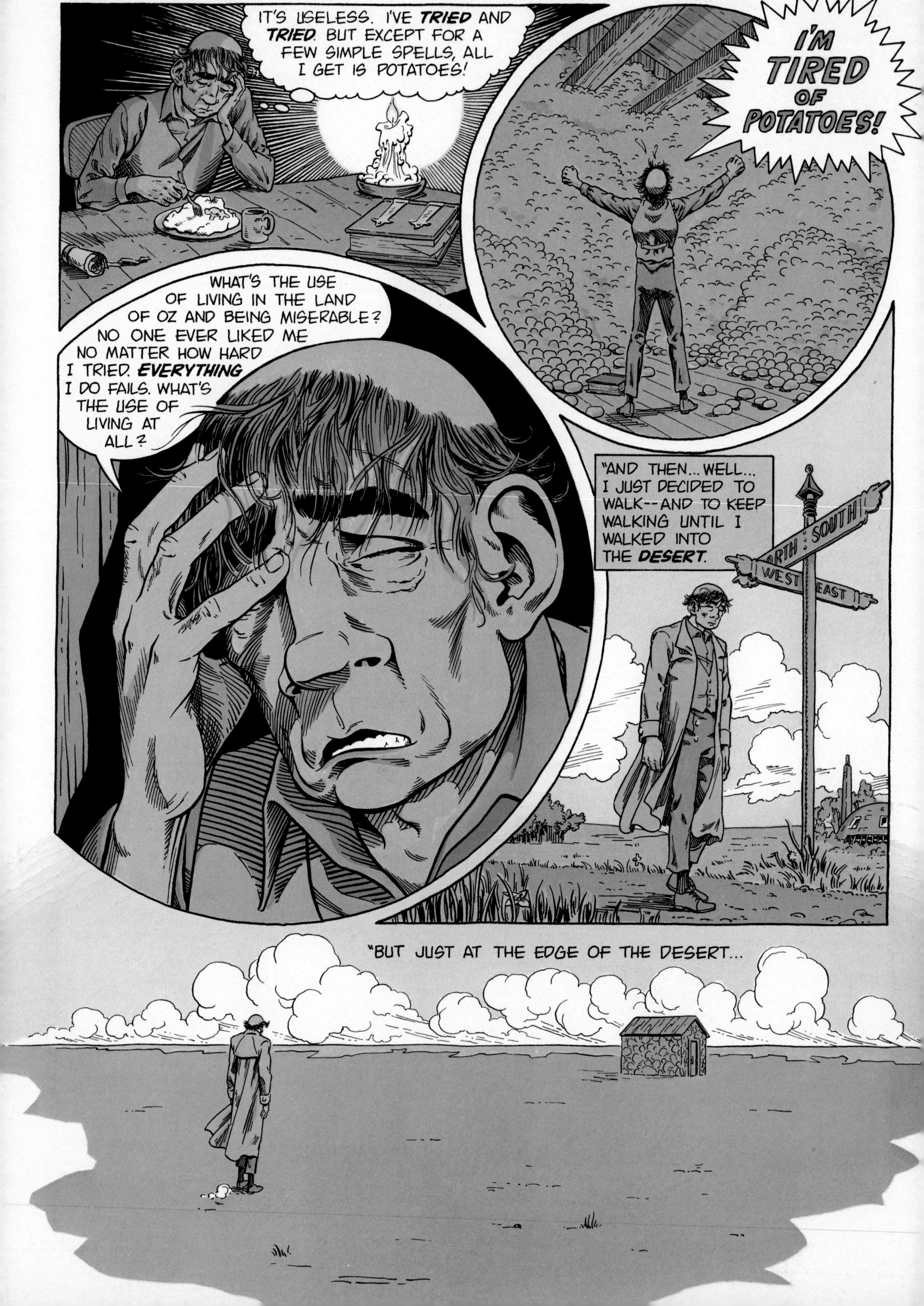
IT'S USELESS. I'VE TRIED AND TRIED. BUT EXCEPT FOR A FEW SIMPLE SPELLS, ALL I GET IS POTATOES!
I'M TIRED OF POTATOES!
WHAT'S THE USE OF LIVING IN THE LAND OF OZ AND BEING MISERABLE? NO ONE EVER LIKED ME NO MATTER HOW HARD I TRIED. EVERYTHING I DO FAILS. WHAT'S THE USE OF LIVING AT ALL?
"AND THEN... WELL... I JUST DECIDED TO WALK--AND TO KEEP WALKING UNTIL I WALKED INTO THE DESERT.
SOUTH
WEST
EAST
"BUT JUST AT THE EDGE OF THE DESERT...

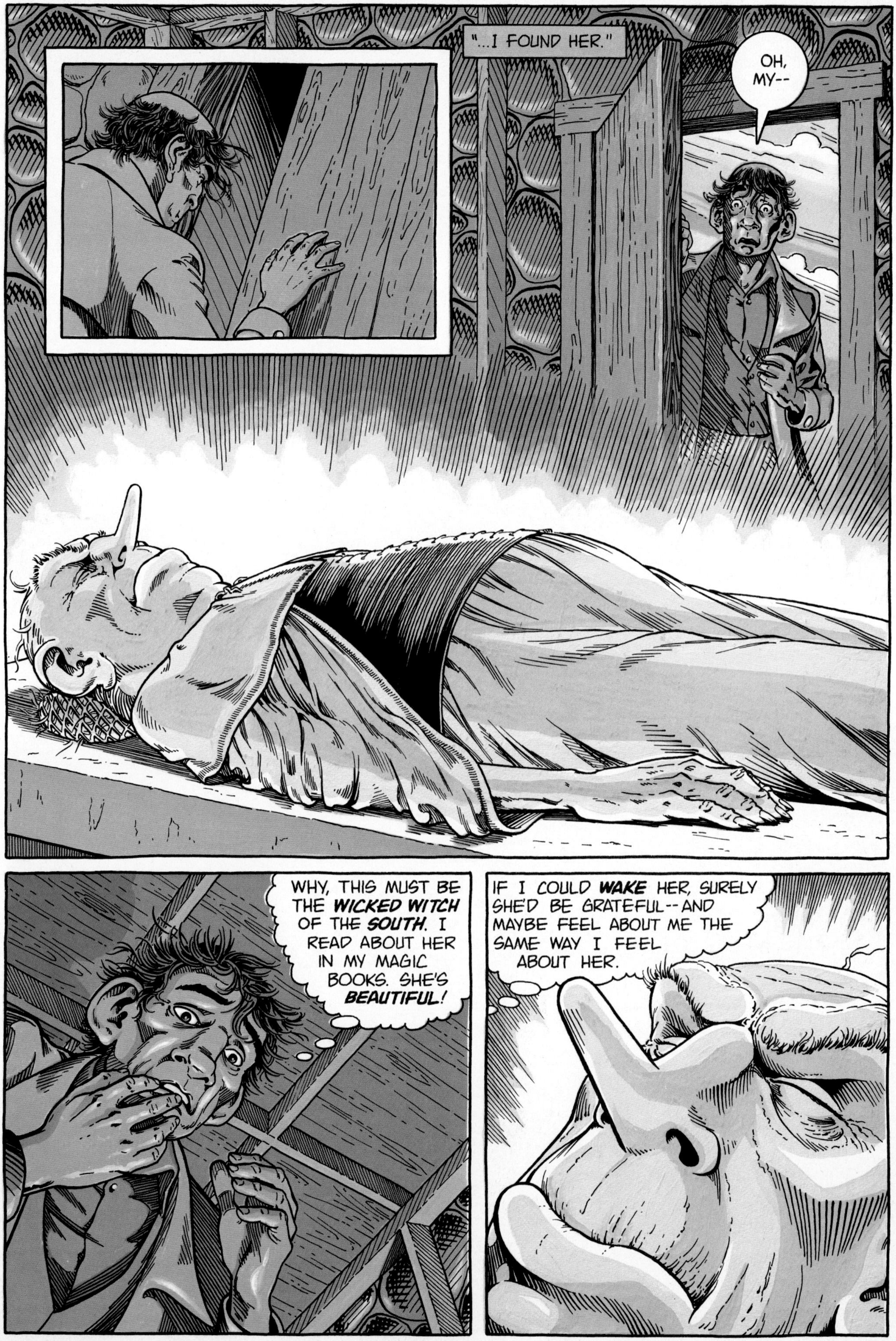
"...I FOUND HER."
OH, MY--
WHY, THIS MUST BE THE **WICKED WITCH** OF THE **SOUTH**. I READ ABOUT HER IN MY MAGIC BOOKS. SHE'S ***BEAUTIFUL!***
IF I COULD **WAKE** HER, SURELY SHE'D BE GRATEFUL--AND MAYBE FEEL ABOUT ME THE SAME WAY I FEEL ABOUT HER.

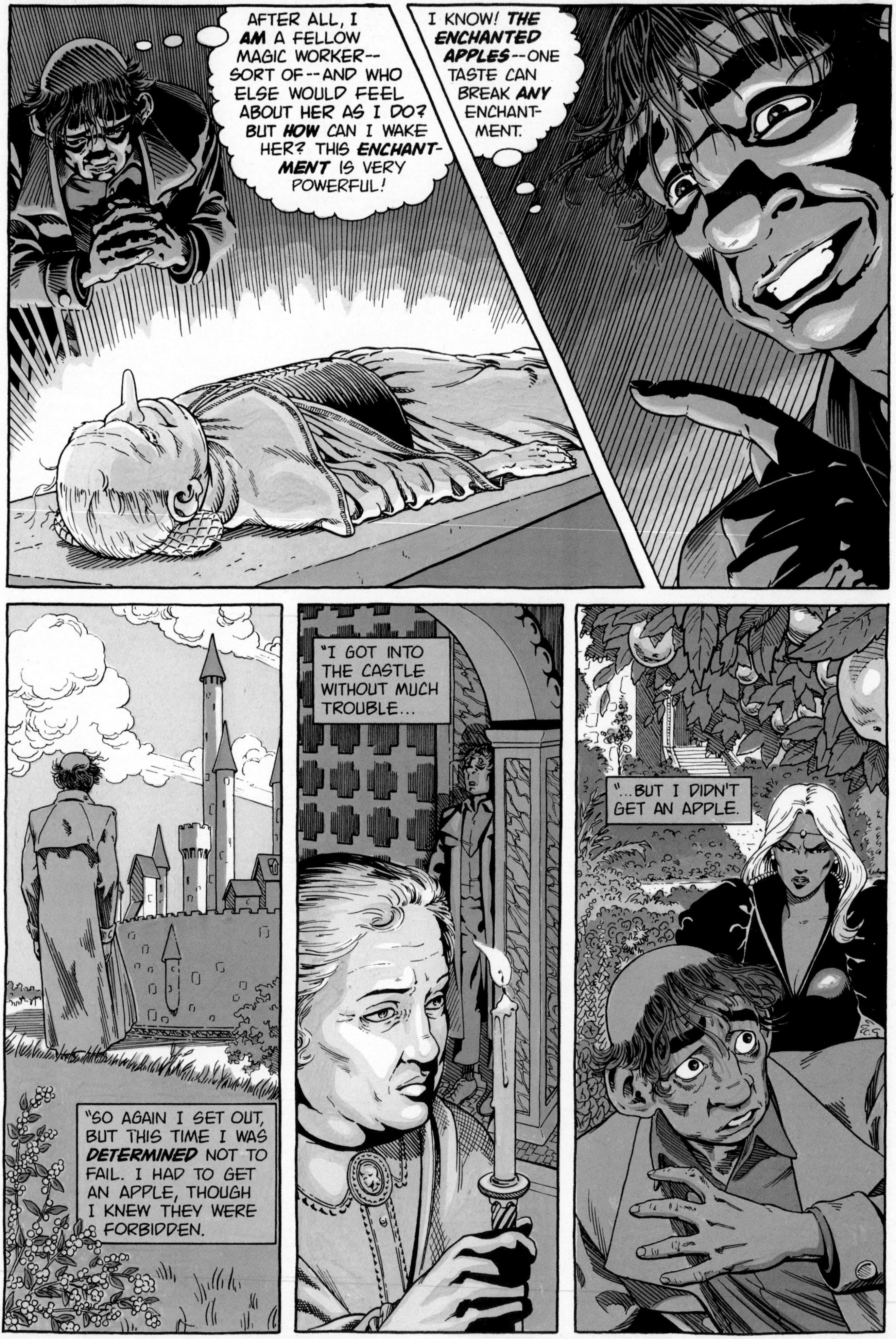
AFTER ALL, I **AM** A FELLOW MAGIC WORKER--SORT OF--AND WHO ELSE WOULD FEEL ABOUT HER AS I DO? BUT **HOW** CAN I WAKE HER? THIS **ENCHANTMENT** IS VERY POWERFUL!
I KNOW! **THE ENCHANTED APPLES**--ONE TASTE CAN BREAK **ANY** ENCHANTMENT.
"SO AGAIN I SET OUT, BUT THIS TIME I WAS **DETERMINED** NOT TO FAIL. I HAD TO GET AN APPLE, THOUGH I KNEW THEY WERE FORBIDDEN.
"I GOT INTO THE CASTLE WITHOUT MUCH TROUBLE...
"...BUT I DIDN'T GET AN APPLE.

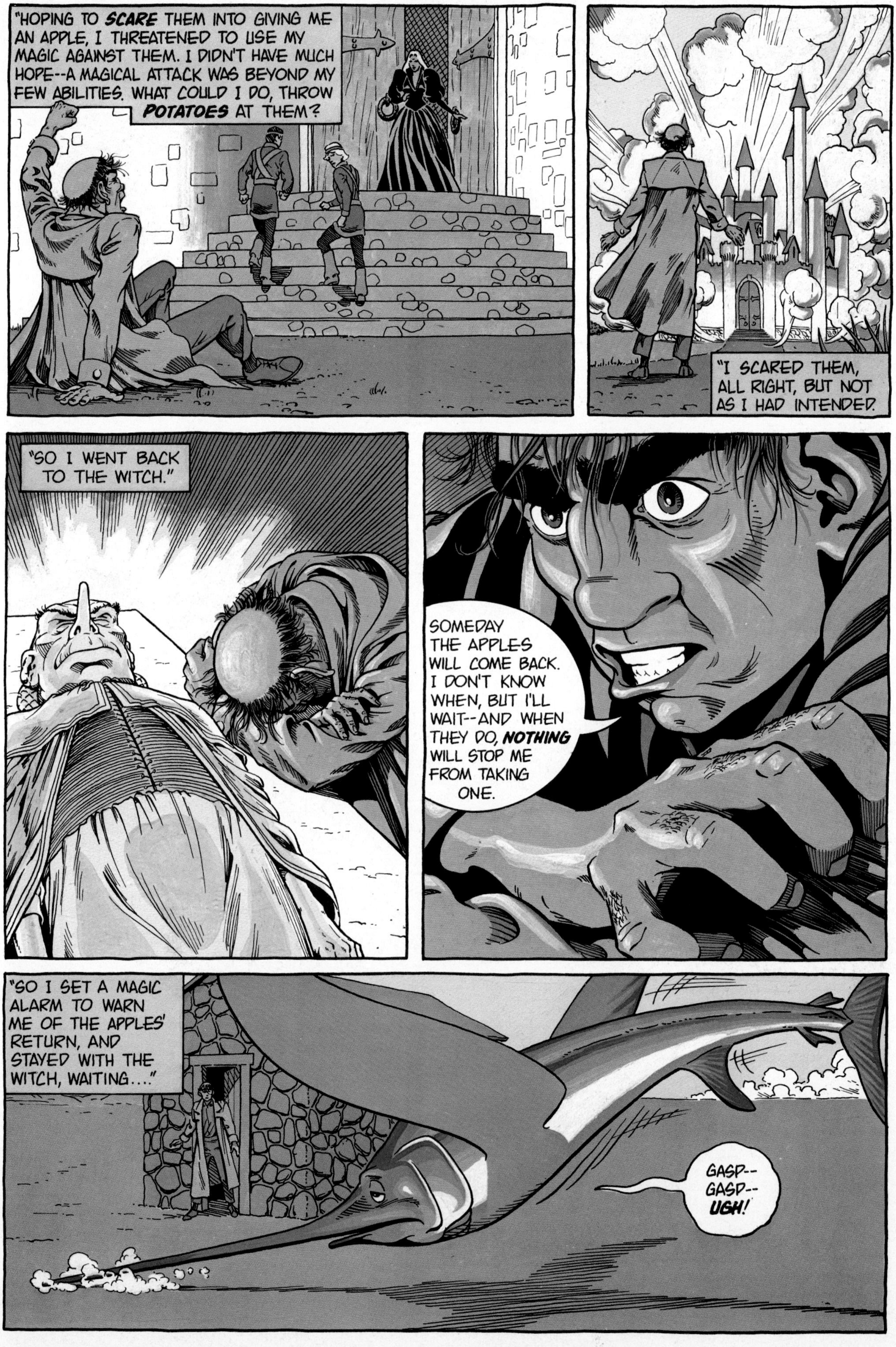
"HOPING TO SCARE THEM INTO GIVING ME AN APPLE, I THREATENED TO USE MY MAGIC AGAINST THEM. I DIDN'T HAVE MUCH HOPE--A MAGICAL ATTACK WAS BEYOND MY FEW ABILITIES. WHAT COULD I DO, THROW POTATOES AT THEM?
"I SCARED THEM, ALL RIGHT, BUT NOT AS I HAD INTENDED.
"SO I WENT BACK TO THE WITCH."
SOMEDAY THE APPLES WILL COME BACK. I DON'T KNOW WHEN, BUT I'LL WAIT--AND WHEN THEY DO, NOTHING WILL STOP ME FROM TAKING ONE.
"SO I SET A MAGIC ALARM TO WARN ME OF THE APPLES' RETURN, AND STAYED WITH THE WITCH, WAITING...."
GASP-- GASP-- UGH!

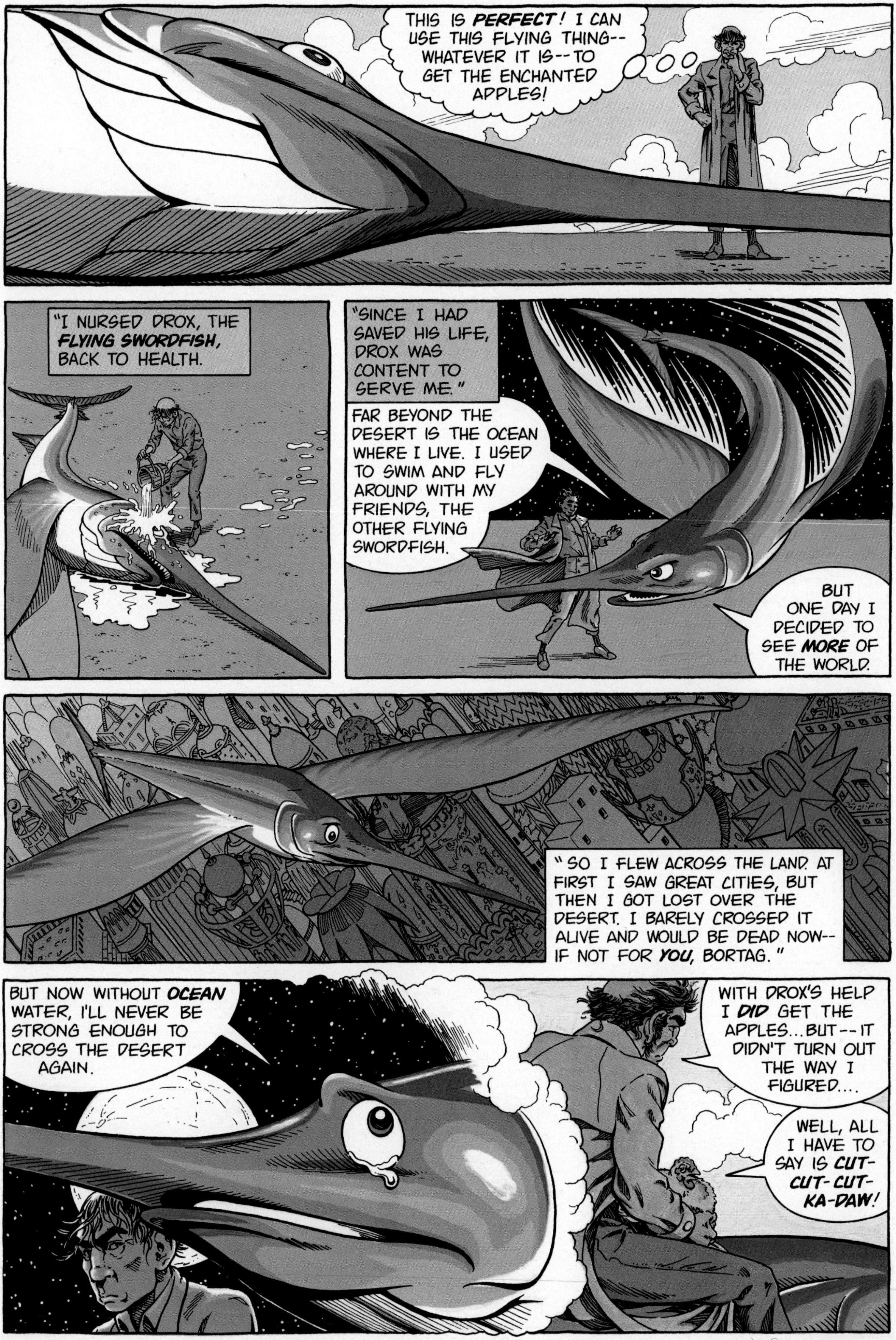
THIS IS PERFECT! I CAN USE THIS FLYING THING-- WHATEVER IT IS--TO GET THE ENCHANTED APPLES!
"I NURSED DROX, THE FLYING SWORDFISH, BACK TO HEALTH.
"SINCE I HAD SAVED HIS LIFE, DROX WAS CONTENT TO SERVE ME."
FAR BEYOND THE DESERT IS THE OCEAN WHERE I LIVE. I USED TO SWIM AND FLY AROUND WITH MY FRIENDS, THE OTHER FLYING SWORDFISH.
BUT ONE DAY I DECIDED TO SEE MORE OF THE WORLD.
" SO I FLEW ACROSS THE LAND. AT FIRST I SAW GREAT CITIES, BUT THEN I GOT LOST OVER THE DESERT. I BARELY CROSSED IT ALIVE AND WOULD BE DEAD NOW-- IF NOT FOR YOU, BORTAG."
BUT NOW WITHOUT OCEAN WATER, I'LL NEVER BE STRONG ENOUGH TO CROSS THE DESERT AGAIN.
WITH DROX'S HELP I DID GET THE APPLES...BUT--IT DIDN'T TURN OUT THE WAY I FIGURED....
WELL, ALL I HAVE TO SAY IS CUT-CUT-CUT-KA-DAW!

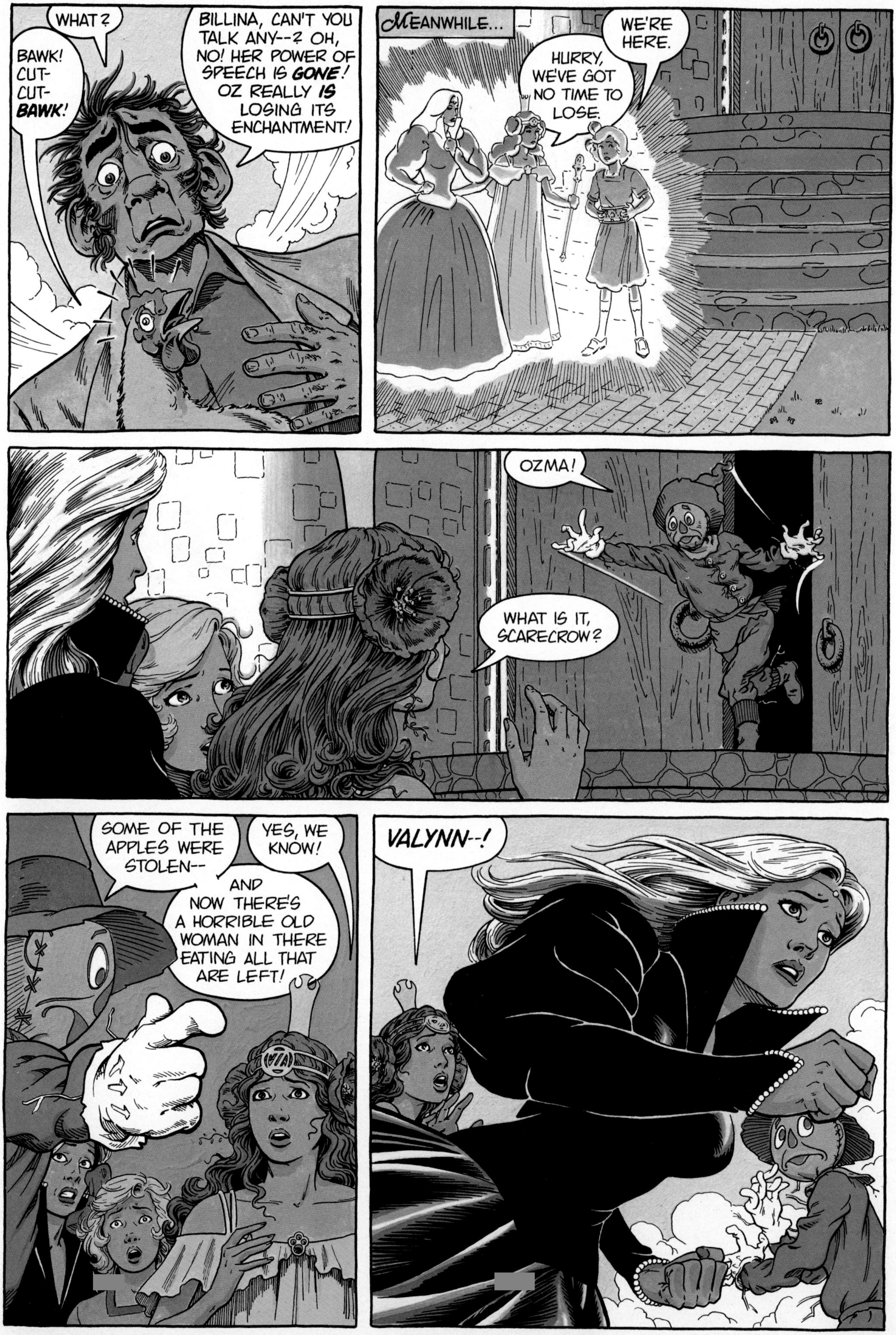
WHAT?
BAWK! CUT-CUT-BAWK!
BILLINA, CAN'T YOU TALK ANY--? OH, NO! HER POWER OF SPEECH IS GONE! OZ REALLY IS LOSING ITS ENCHANTMENT!
MEANWHILE...
HURRY, WE'VE GOT NO TIME TO LOSE.
WE'RE HERE.
OZMA!
WHAT IS IT, SCARECROW?
SOME OF THE APPLES WERE STOLEN--
YES, WE KNOW!
AND NOW THERE'S A HORRIBLE OLD WOMAN IN THERE EATING ALL THAT ARE LEFT!
VALYNN--!

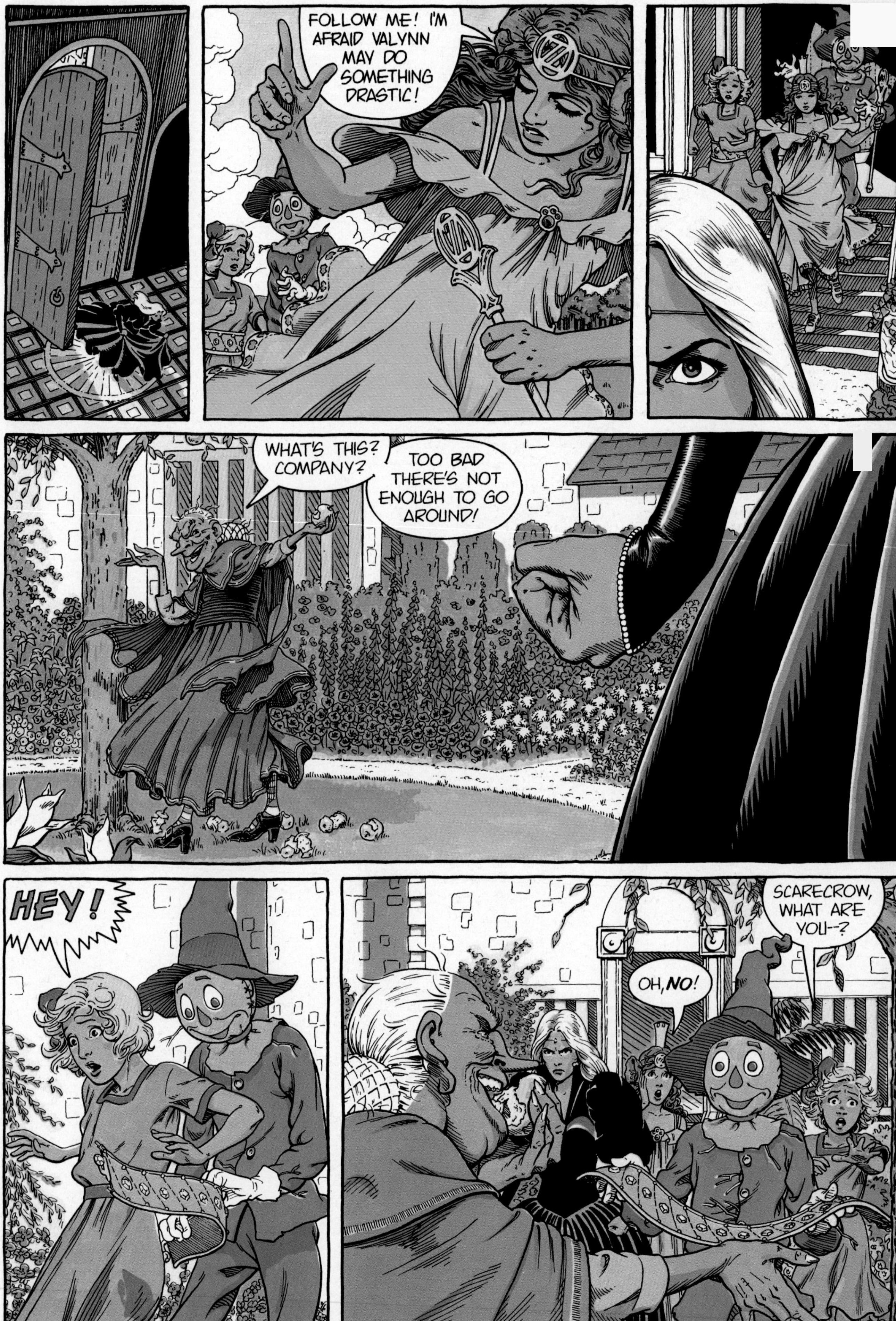
FOLLOW ME! I'M AFRAID VALYNN MAY DO SOMETHING DRASTIC!
WHAT'S THIS? COMPANY?
TOO BAD THERE'S NOT ENOUGH TO GO AROUND!
HEY!
SCARECROW, WHAT ARE YOU--?
OH, NO!

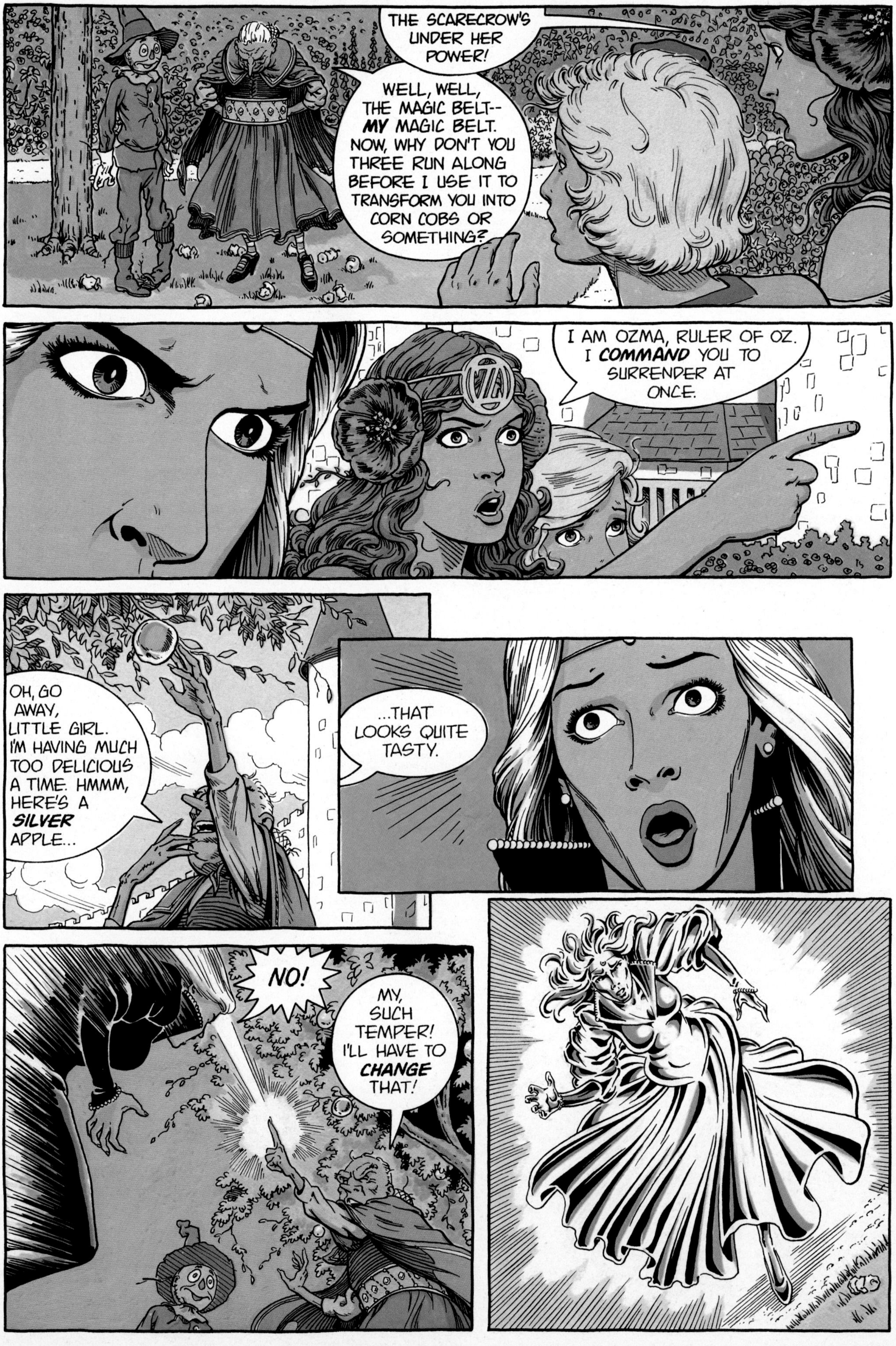
THE SCARECROW'S UNDER HER POWER!
WELL, WELL, THE MAGIC BELT-- ***MY*** MAGIC BELT. NOW, WHY DON'T YOU THREE RUN ALONG BEFORE I USE IT TO TRANSFORM YOU INTO CORN COBS OR SOMETHING?
I AM OZMA, RULER OF OZ. I ***COMMAND*** YOU TO SURRENDER AT ONCE.
OH, GO AWAY, LITTLE GIRL. I'M HAVING MUCH TOO DELICIOUS A TIME. HMMM, HERE'S A ***SILVER*** APPLE...
...THAT LOOKS QUITE TASTY.
NO!
MY, SUCH TEMPER! I'LL HAVE TO ***CHANGE*** THAT!

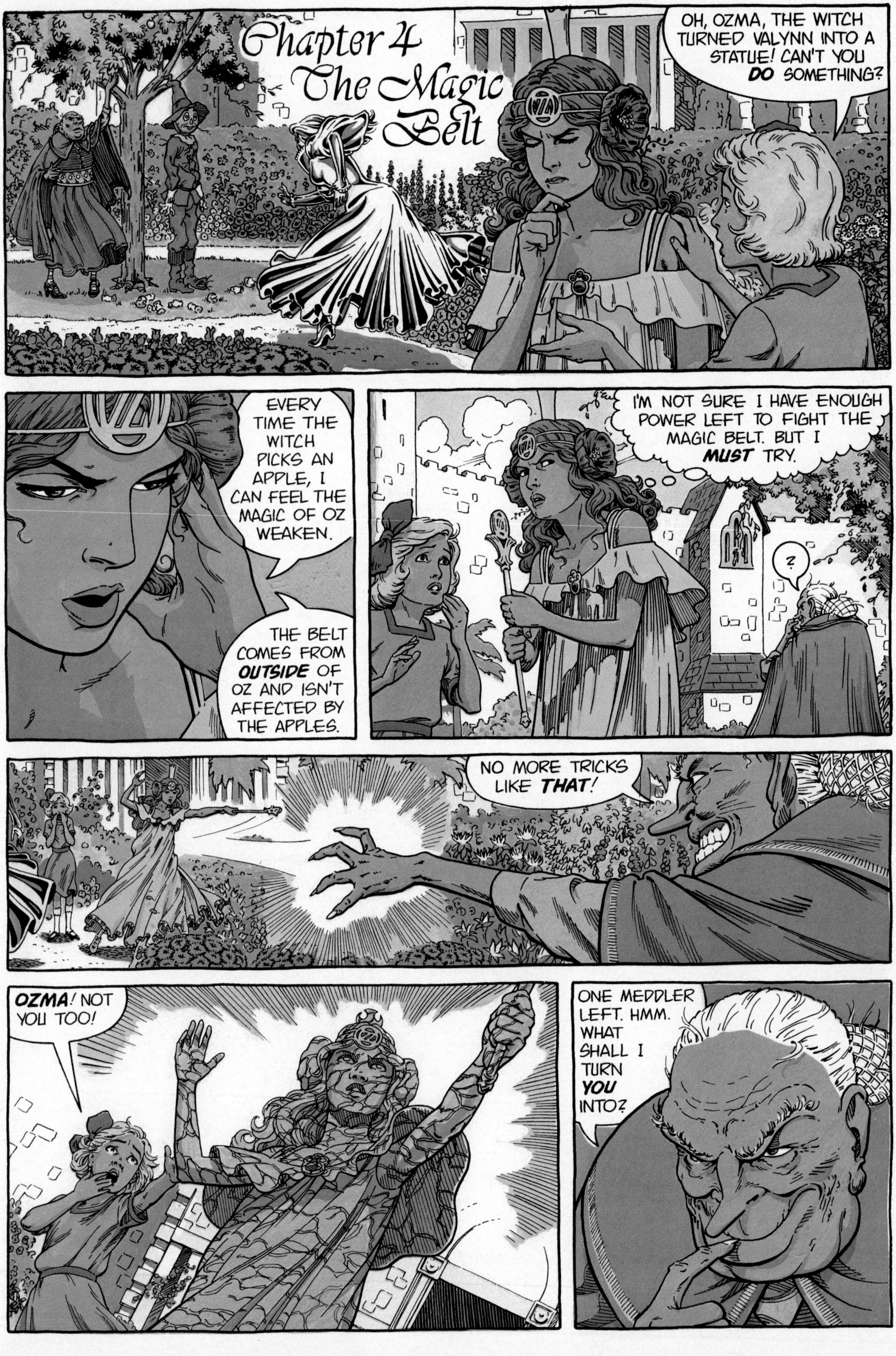
Chapter 4
The Magic Belt
OH, OZMA, THE WITCH TURNED VALYNN INTO A STATUE! CAN'T YOU DO SOMETHING?
EVERY TIME THE WITCH PICKS AN APPLE, I CAN FEEL THE MAGIC OF OZ WEAKEN.
THE BELT COMES FROM OUTSIDE OF OZ AND ISN'T AFFECTED BY THE APPLES.
I'M NOT SURE I HAVE ENOUGH POWER LEFT TO FIGHT THE MAGIC BELT. BUT I MUST TRY.
?
NO MORE TRICKS LIKE THAT!
OZMA! NOT YOU TOO!
ONE MEDDLER LEFT. HMM. WHAT SHALL I TURN YOU INTO?

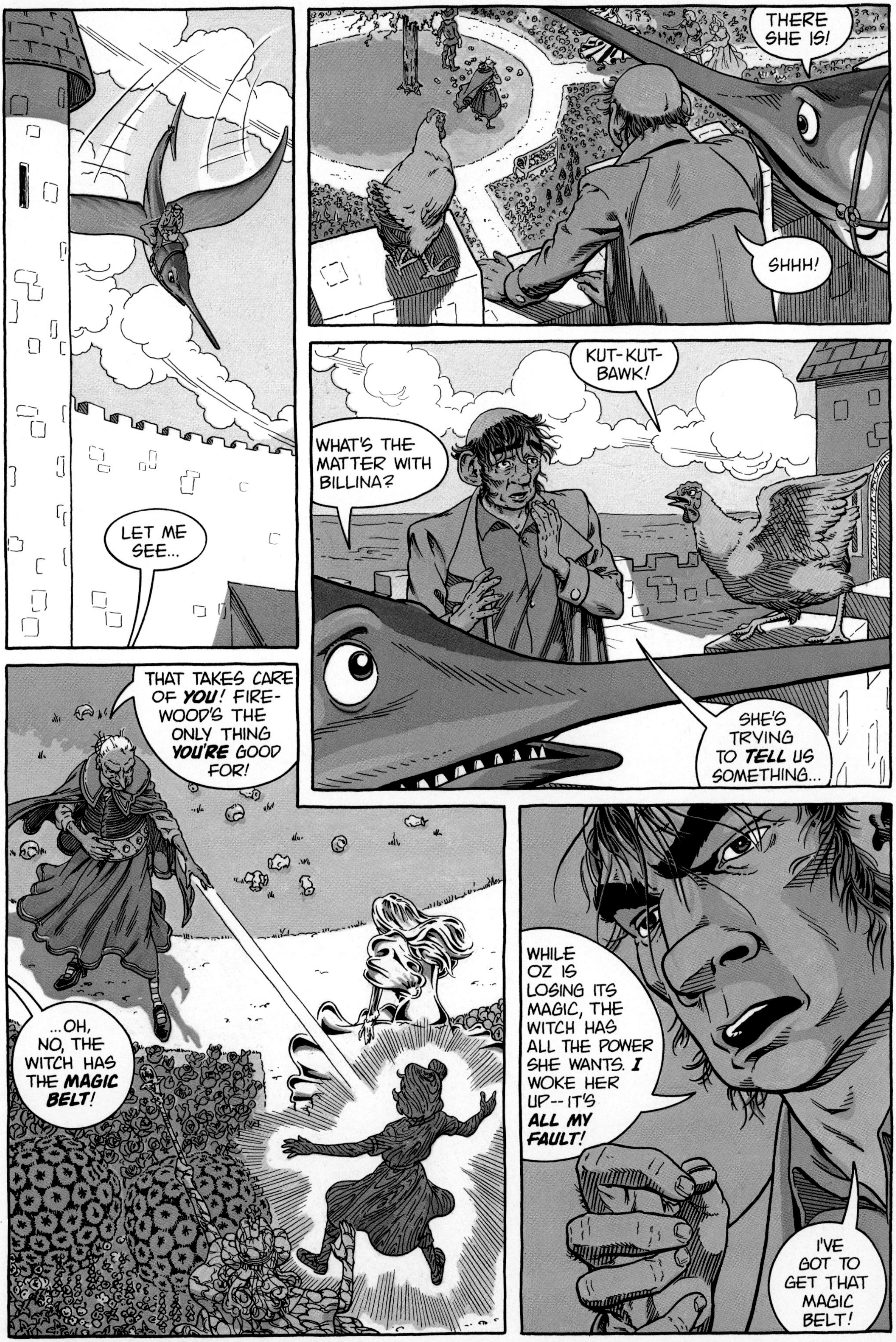
LET ME SEE...
THERE SHE IS!
SHHH!
KUT-KUT-BAWK!
WHAT'S THE MATTER WITH BILLINA?
SHE'S TRYING TO TELL US SOMETHING...
THAT TAKES CARE OF YOU! FIRE-WOOD'S THE ONLY THING YOU'RE GOOD FOR!
...OH, NO, THE WITCH HAS THE MAGIC BELT!
WHILE OZ IS LOSING ITS MAGIC, THE WITCH HAS ALL THE POWER SHE WANTS. I WOKE HER UP-- IT'S ALL MY FAULT!
I'VE GOT TO GET THAT MAGIC BELT!

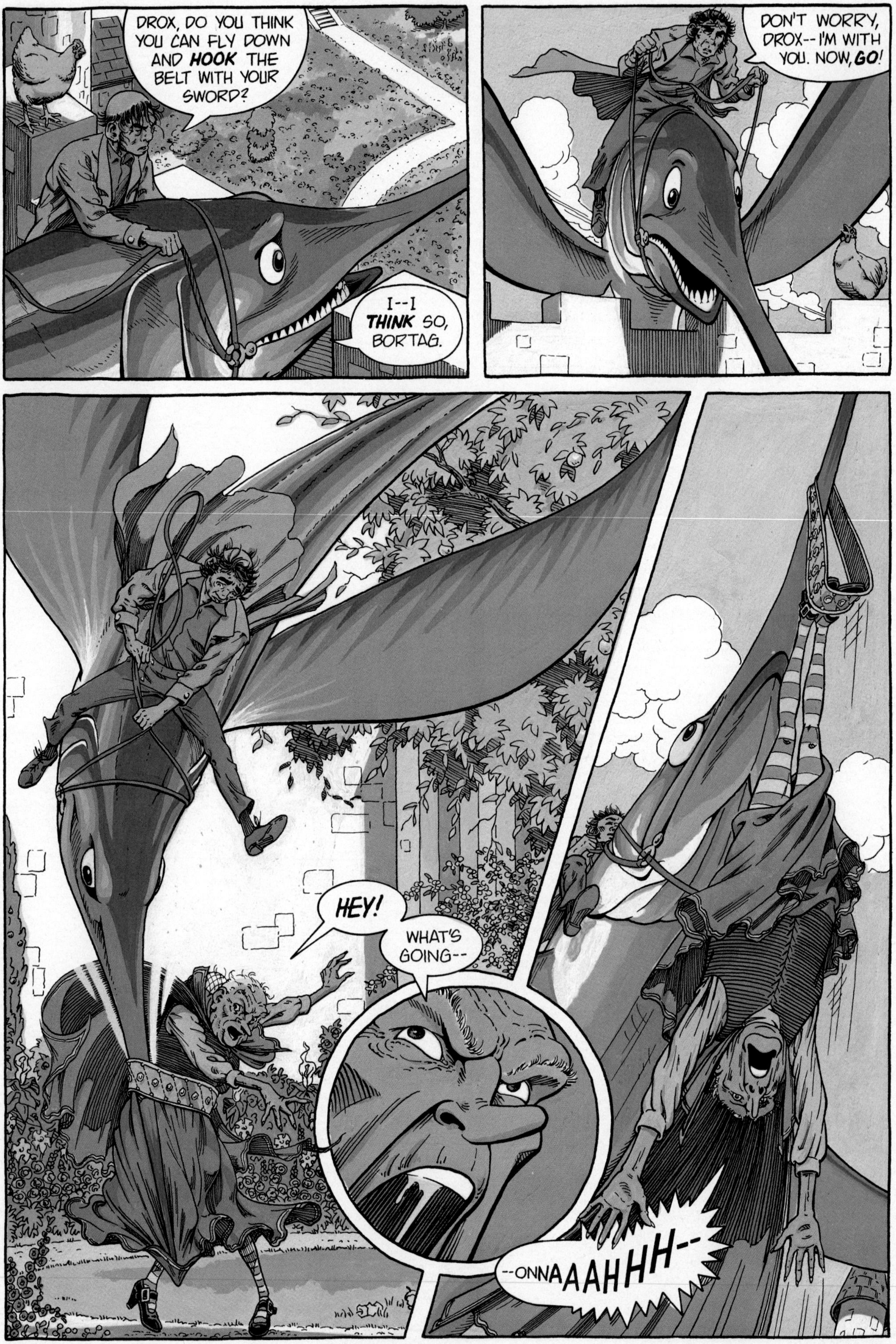
DROX, DO YOU THINK YOU CAN FLY DOWN AND **HOOK** THE BELT WITH YOUR SWORD?
I--I **THINK** SO, BORTAG.
DON'T WORRY, DROX--I'M WITH YOU. NOW, **GO**!
HEY!
WHAT'S GOING--
--ONNAAAHHH--

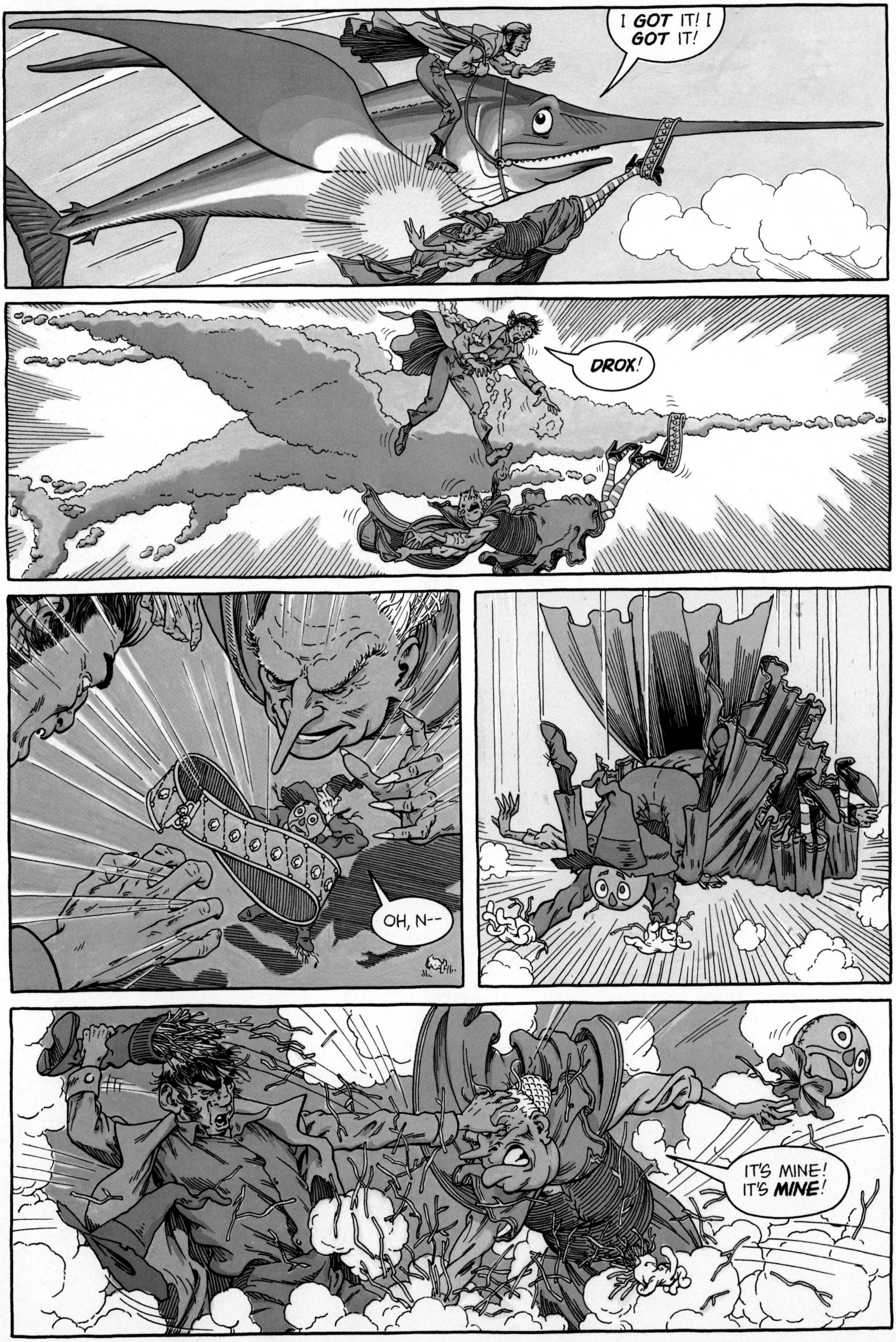
I GOT IT! I GOT IT!
DROX!
OH, N--
IT'S MINE! IT'S MINE!

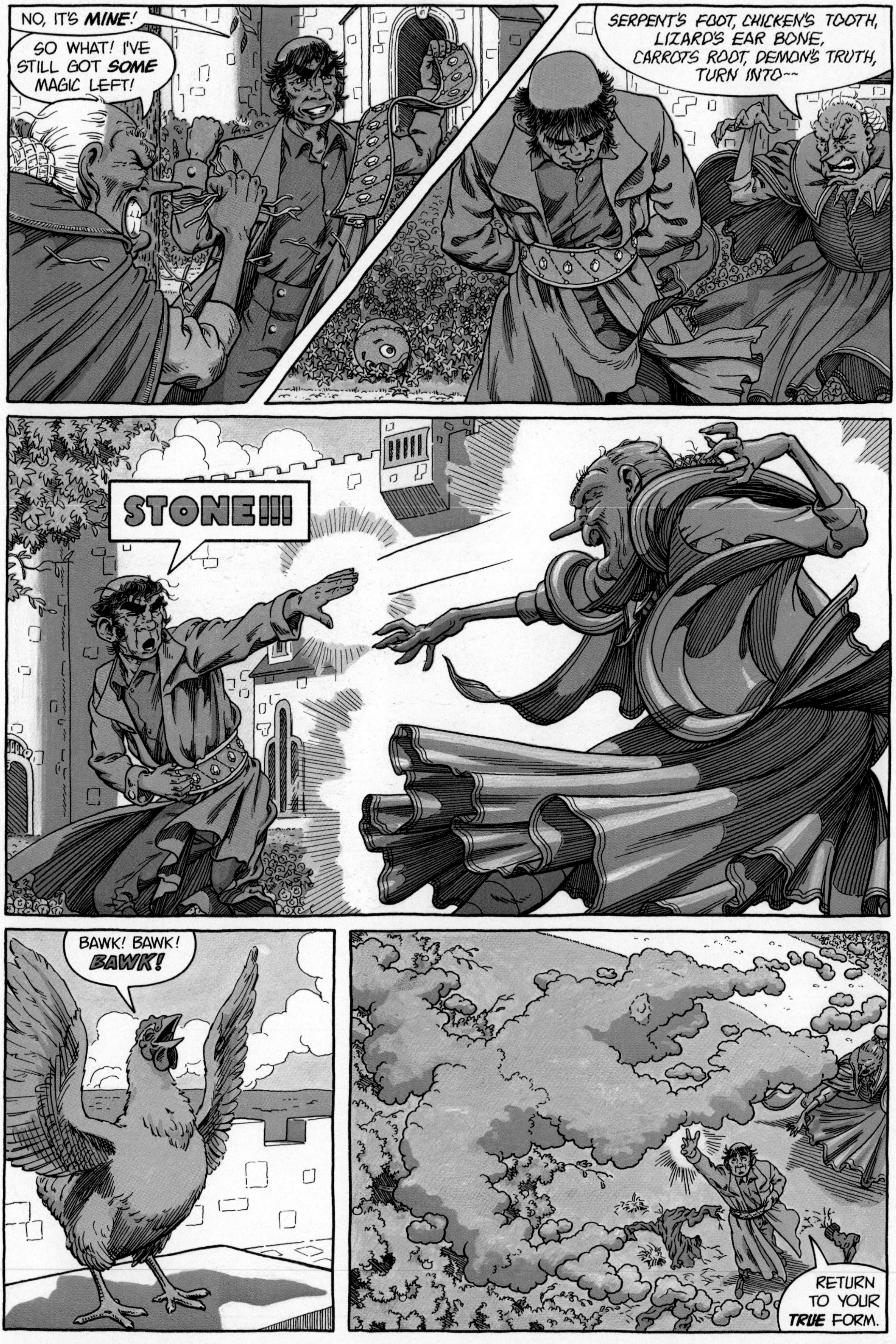
NO, IT'S **MINE**!
SO WHAT! I'VE STILL GOT **SOME** MAGIC LEFT!
SERPENT'S FOOT, CHICKEN'S TOOTH, LIZARD'S EAR BONE, CARROTS ROOT, DEMON'S TRUTH, TURN INTO--
STONE!!!
BAWK! BAWK! **BAWK!**
RETURN TO YOUR **TRUE** FORM.

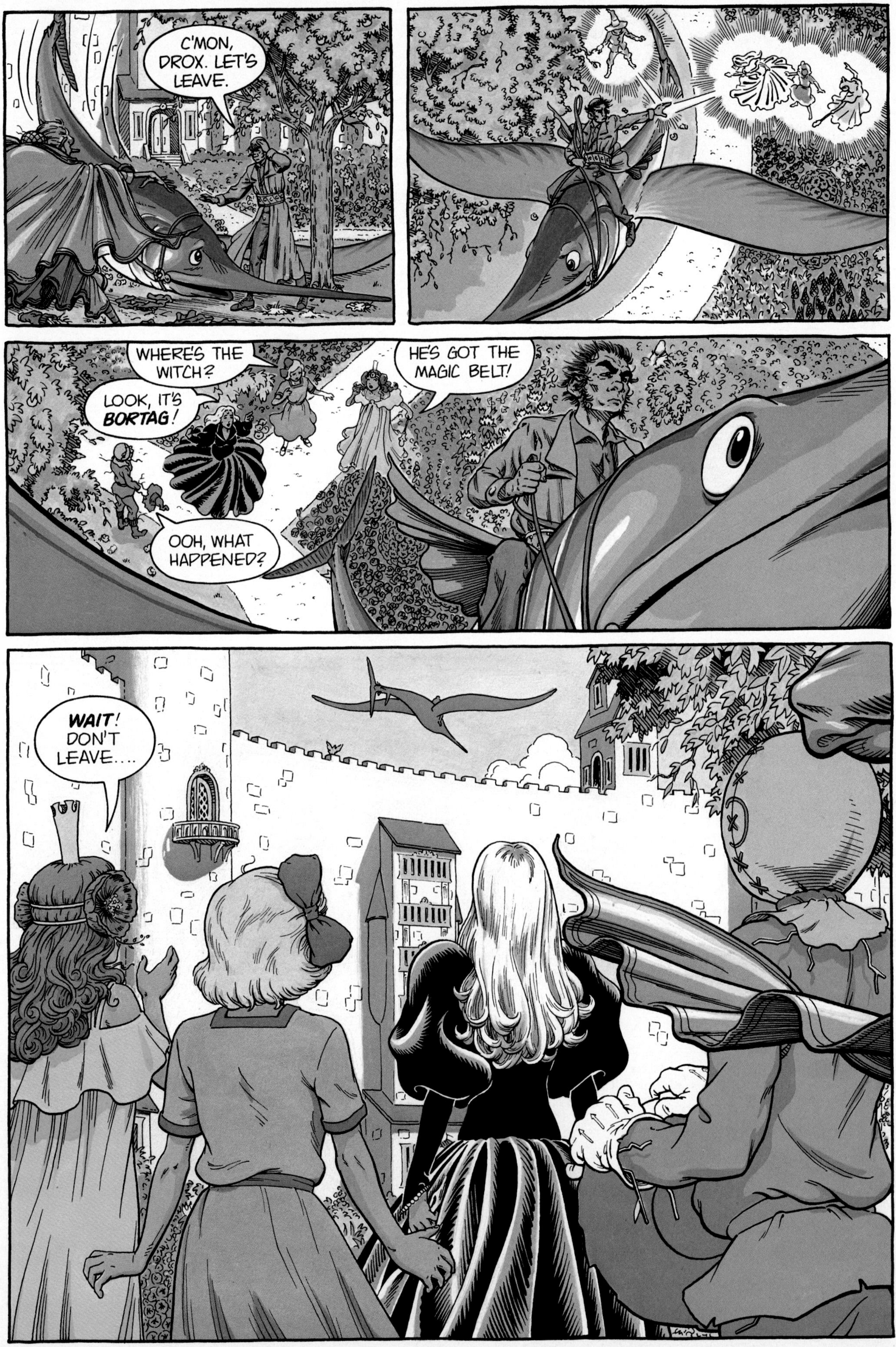
C'MON, DROX. LET'S LEAVE.
WHERE'S THE WITCH?
LOOK, IT'S **BORTAG**!
HE'S GOT THE MAGIC BELT!
OOH, WHAT HAPPENED?
WAIT! DON'T LEAVE....

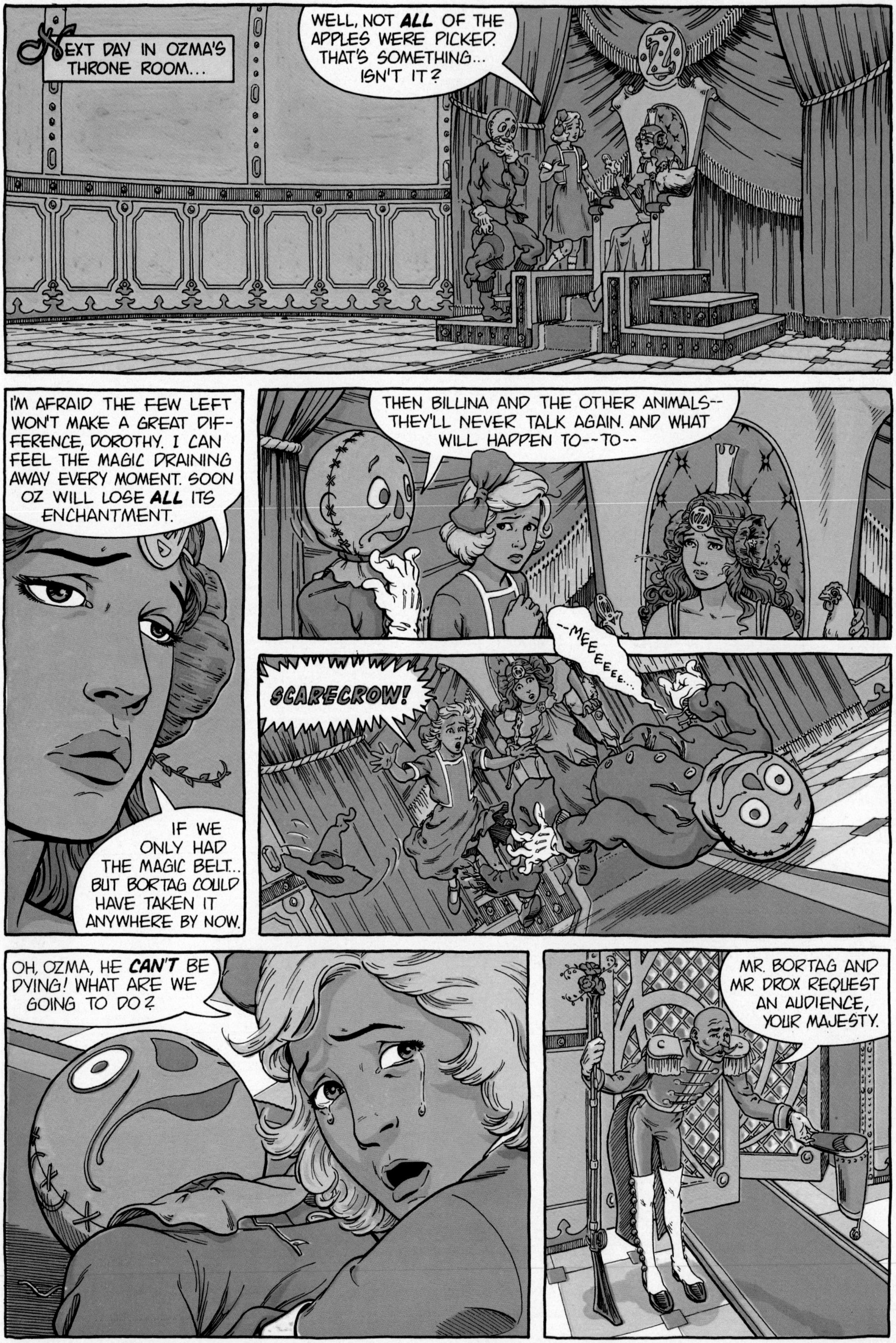
NEXT DAY IN OZMA'S THRONE ROOM...
WELL, NOT ALL OF THE APPLES WERE PICKED. THAT'S SOMETHING... ISN'T IT?
I'M AFRAID THE FEW LEFT WON'T MAKE A GREAT DIFFERENCE, DOROTHY. I CAN FEEL THE MAGIC DRAINING AWAY EVERY MOMENT. SOON OZ WILL LOSE ALL ITS ENCHANTMENT.
THEN BILLINA AND THE OTHER ANIMALS-- THEY'LL NEVER TALK AGAIN. AND WHAT WILL HAPPEN TO--TO--
--MEEEEEE...
SCARECROW!
IF WE ONLY HAD THE MAGIC BELT... BUT BORTAG COULD HAVE TAKEN IT ANYWHERE BY NOW.
OH, OZMA, HE CAN'T BE DYING! WHAT ARE WE GOING TO DO?
MR. BORTAG AND MR. DROX REQUEST AN AUDIENCE, YOUR MAJESTY.

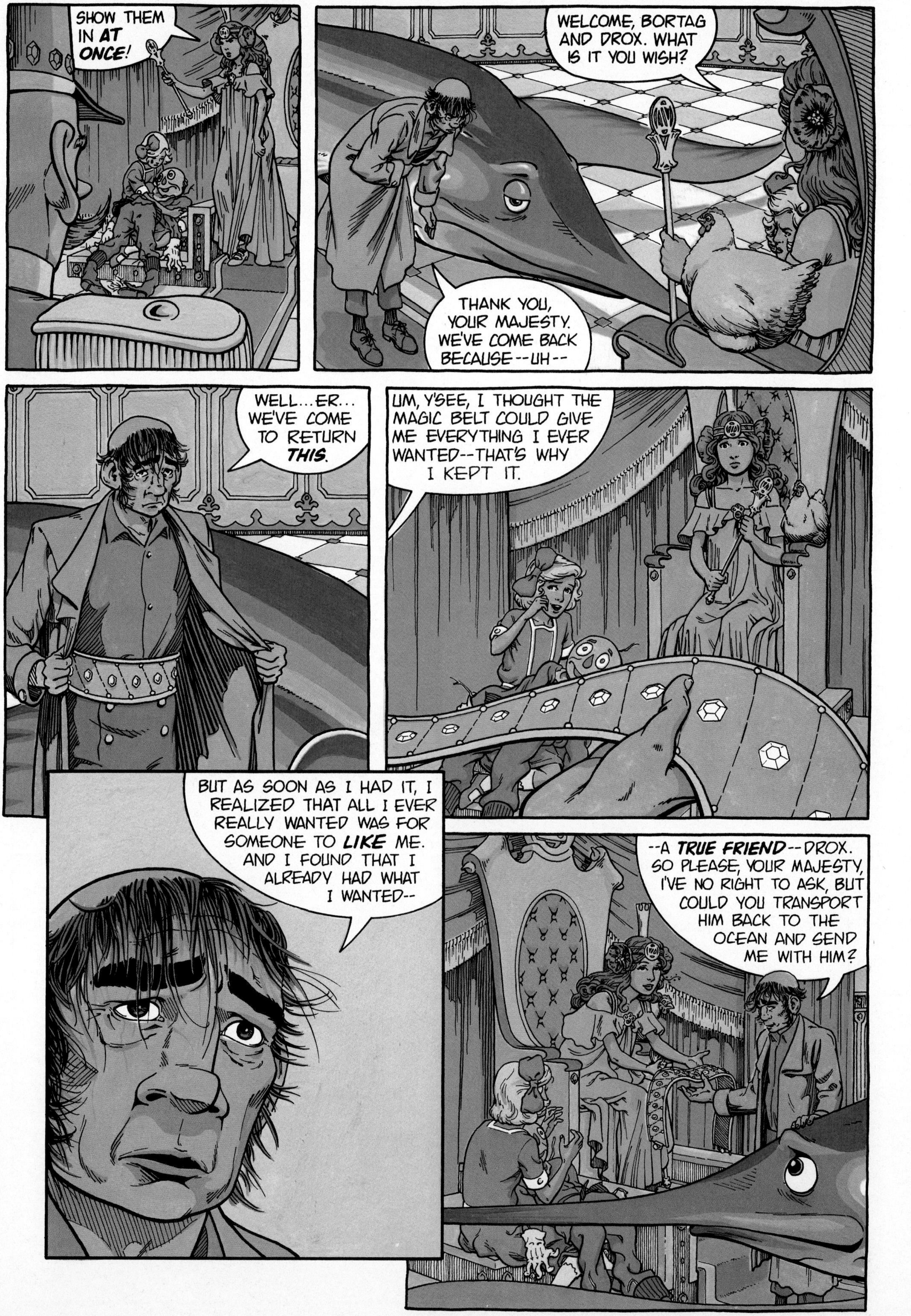
SHOW THEM IN AT ONCE!
WELCOME, BORTAG AND DROX. WHAT IS IT YOU WISH?
THANK YOU, YOUR MAJESTY. WE'VE COME BACK BECAUSE--UH--
WELL...ER... WE'VE COME TO RETURN THIS.
UM, Y'SEE, I THOUGHT THE MAGIC BELT COULD GIVE ME EVERYTHING I EVER WANTED--THAT'S WHY I KEPT IT.
BUT AS SOON AS I HAD IT, I REALIZED THAT ALL I EVER REALLY WANTED WAS FOR SOMEONE TO LIKE ME. AND I FOUND THAT I ALREADY HAD WHAT I WANTED--
--A TRUE FRIEND--DROX. SO PLEASE, YOUR MAJESTY, I'VE NO RIGHT TO ASK, BUT COULD YOU TRANSPORT HIM BACK TO THE OCEAN AND SEND ME WITH HIM?

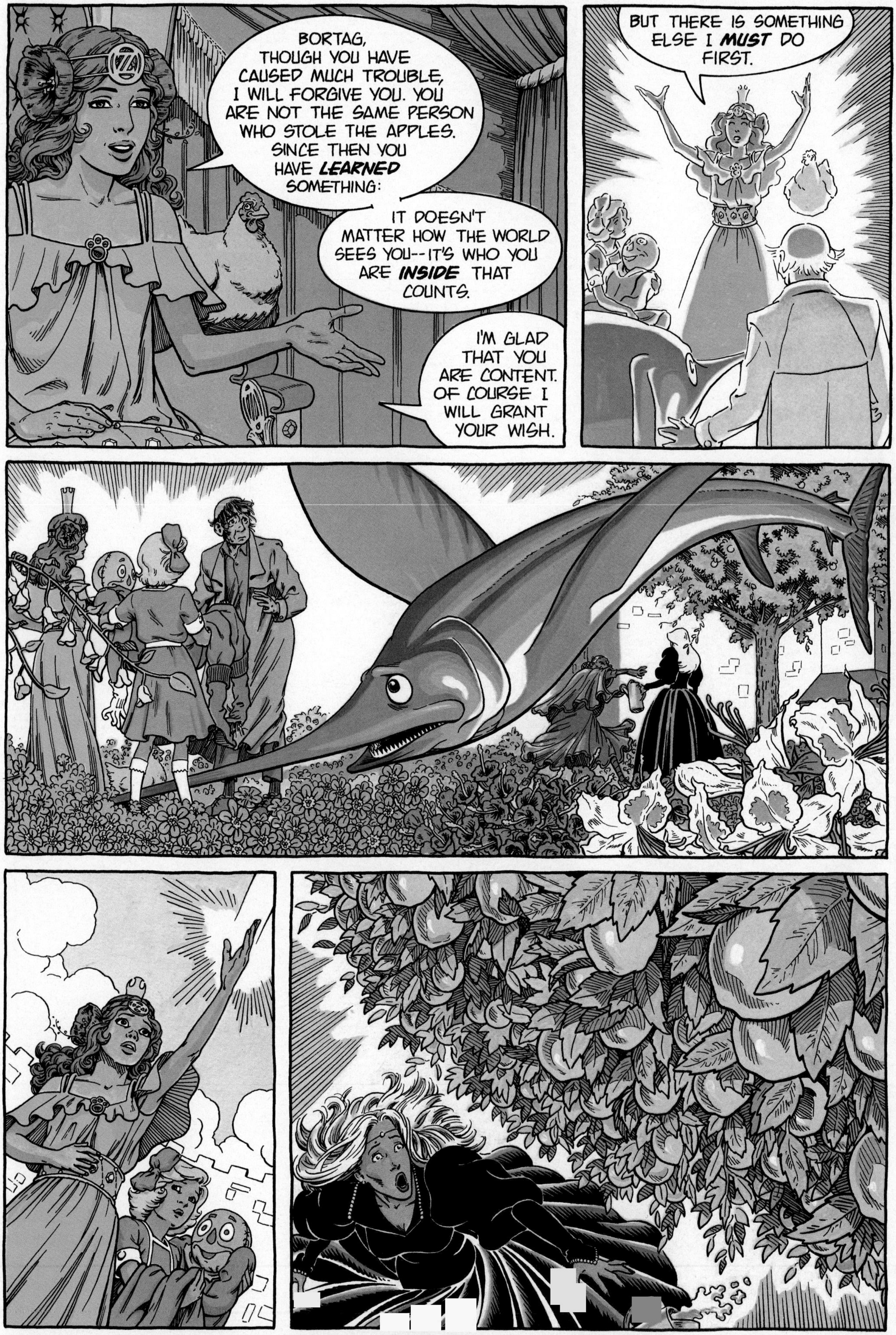
BORTAG, THOUGH YOU HAVE CAUSED MUCH TROUBLE, I WILL FORGIVE YOU. YOU ARE NOT THE SAME PERSON WHO STOLE THE APPLES. SINCE THEN YOU HAVE LEARNED SOMETHING:
IT DOESN'T MATTER HOW THE WORLD SEES YOU--IT'S WHO YOU ARE INSIDE THAT COUNTS.
I'M GLAD THAT YOU ARE CONTENT. OF COURSE I WILL GRANT YOUR WISH.
BUT THERE IS SOMETHING ELSE I MUST DO FIRST.

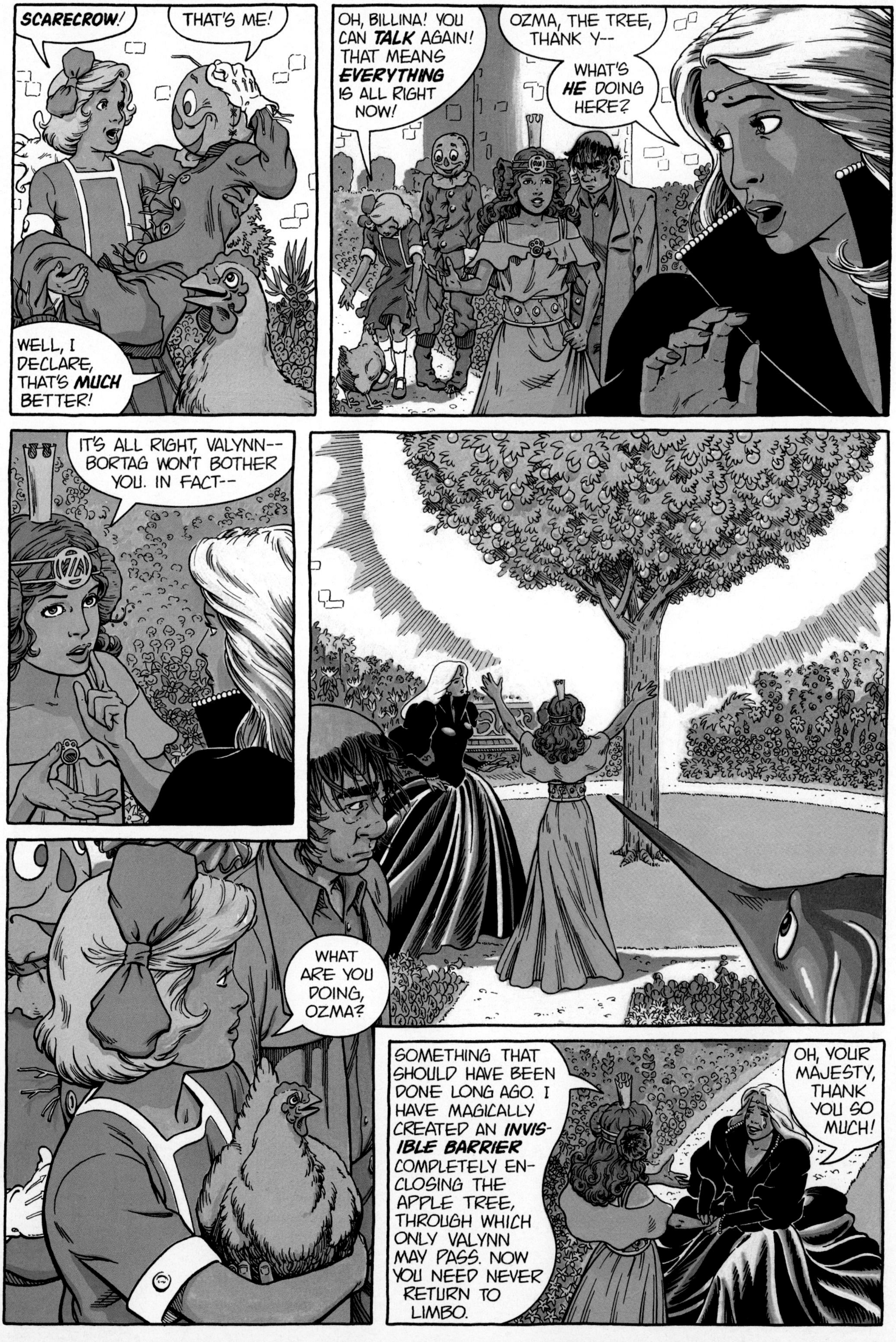

SCARECROW!
THAT'S ME!
WELL, I DECLARE, THAT'S MUCH BETTER!
OH, BILLINA! YOU CAN TALK AGAIN! THAT MEANS EVERYTHING IS ALL RIGHT NOW!
OZMA, THE TREE, THANK Y--
WHAT'S HE DOING HERE?
IT'S ALL RIGHT, VALYNN-- BORTAG WON'T BOTHER YOU. IN FACT--
WHAT ARE YOU DOING, OZMA?
SOMETHING THAT SHOULD HAVE BEEN DONE LONG AGO. I HAVE MAGICALLY CREATED AN INVISIBLE BARRIER COMPLETELY ENCLOSING THE APPLE TREE, THROUGH WHICH ONLY VALYNN MAY PASS. NOW YOU NEED NEVER RETURN TO LIMBO.
OH, YOUR MAJESTY, THANK YOU SO MUCH!

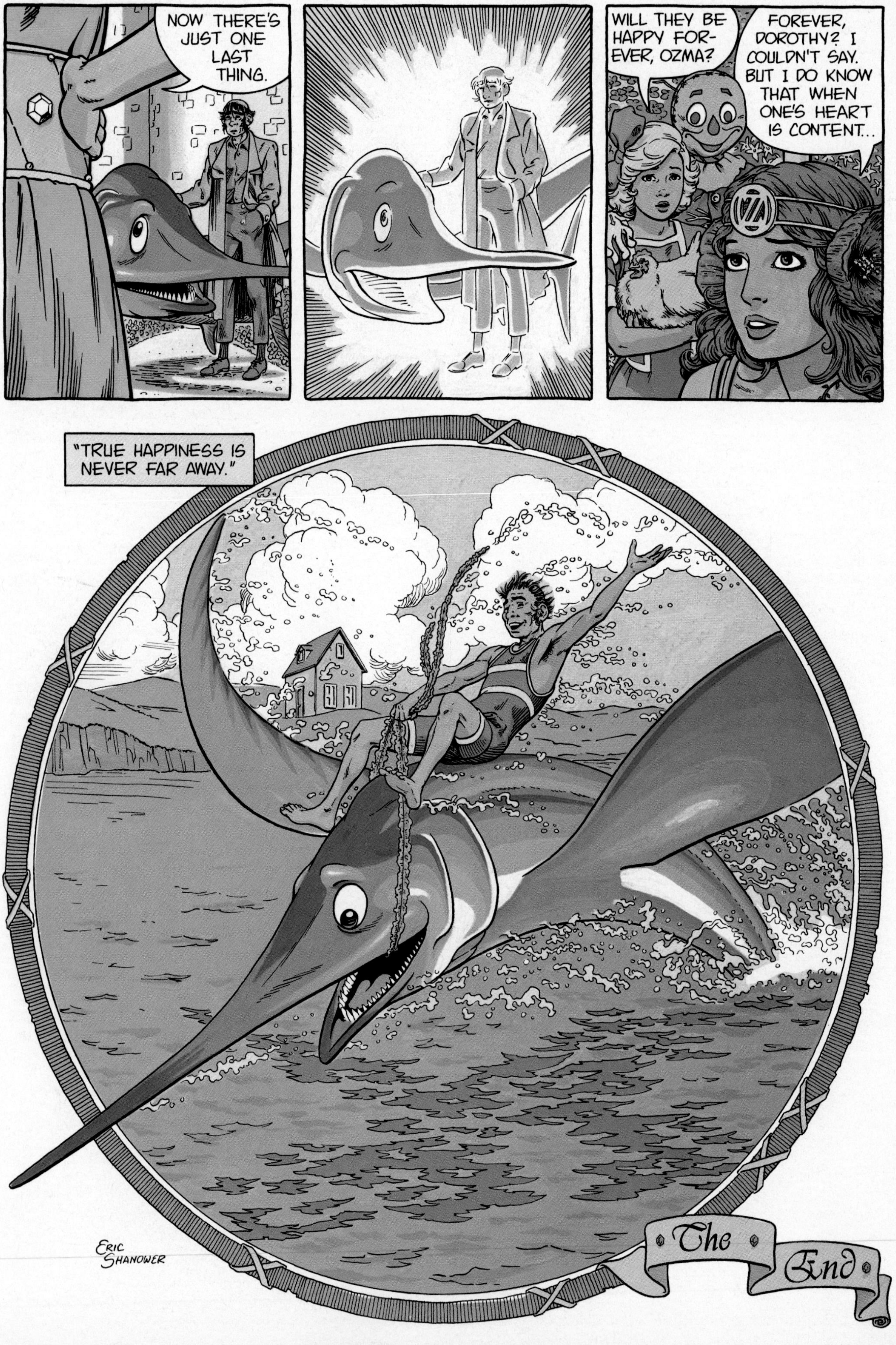
NOW THERE'S JUST ONE LAST THING.
WILL THEY BE HAPPY FOREVER, OZMA?
FOREVER, DOROTHY? I COULDN'T SAY. BUT I DO KNOW THAT WHEN ONE'S HEART IS CONTENT...
"TRUE HAPPINESS IS NEVER FAR AWAY."
ERIC SHANOWER
The End